COUNTRY WALKS
AROUND LONDON

COUNTRY WALKS AROUND LONDON

LEIGH HATTS

with illustrations by
Ken Hatts

David & Charles
Newton Abbot   London
Hippocrene Books Inc
New York

British Library Cataloguing in Publication Data

Hatts, Leigh
   Country walks around London.
   1. London (England)—Description—1951——
   Guide-books
   I. Title
   914.21'04858   DA679

   ISBN 0-7153-8439-2 (Great Britain)
   ISBN 0-88254-834-4 (United States)

Phototypeset by Typesetters (Birmingham) Limited
and printed in Great Britain
by Redwood Burn Limited, Trowbridge
for David & Charles (Publishers) Limited
Brunel House   Newton Abbot   Devon

CONTENTS

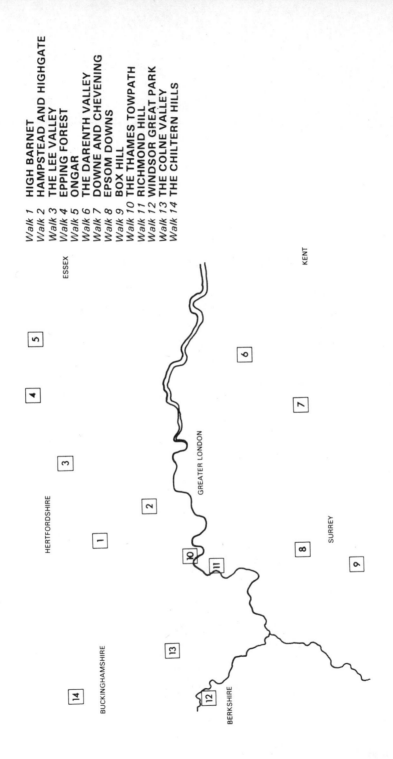

ESSEX

KENT

HERTFORDSHIRE

BUCKINGHAMSHIRE

BERKSHIRE

SURREY

GREATER LONDON

FOREWORD

If you know where to look, you can take a deep breath of fresh air and discover delightful walks in and around the Greater London area. By following footpaths and towpaths or taking to the parks and woodlands, this book guides you through many miles of pleasant countryside. Walking is now Britain's most popular outdoor pastime and here are over 100 miles of pleasant paths which can be found within the pages of a good London A-Z.

An early start for a full country walk is recommended as a race against darkness will spoil the outing. Also, a morning attempt can allow more time for lingering in an old church or resting at a viewpoint. There is much history to be enjoyed, for such figures as Henry VIII, Cromwell and Wesley visited many of the places described and one finds, for example, that the effects of the Great Plague reached far beyond the City. Many villages and towns will therefore warrant further exploration by car or public transport later.

Sketch maps accompany each Walk, but an Ordnance Survey map is desirable and a worthwhile investment as it will help to put a valley or range of hills in its geographical context. OS maps can be borrowed from public libraries. Most spellings used in this book are taken from the OS map; there are inevitable discrepancies between maps and signposts etc.

A good pair of shoes is essential; a long dry walk can have a surprise muddy patch. Also, remember that walking can be a delight in any season and an autumn, winter or spring return to a route first tried in summer can bring new insights into nature.

This need not be an expensive hobby. A pack of sandwiches and a small flask will give one more freedom to walk at a slow pace without having to remember licensing hours — although noted pubs and celebrated tea stalls (on Epsom Downs and at

Burford Bridge) are very tempting. Rail travellers should buy an Awayday ticket (available after about 9.30am and all day at weekends) to the furthest station being used on the line. London Transport offers a cheap maximum fare Underground return ticket on Sundays.

Every effort has been made to ensure that the information given in this book is correct but details are liable to alteration without notice and the author and publishers cannot accept responsibility for any inaccuracies or for those who stray from the footpaths.

THE COUNTRY CODE

Enjoy the countryside and respect its life and work
Guard against all risk of fire
Fasten all gates
Keep your dogs under close control
Keep to public paths across farmland
Use gates and stiles to cross fences, hedges and walls
Leave livestock, crops and machinery alone
Take your litter home
Help to keep all water clean
Protect wildlife, plants and trees
Take special care on country roads
Make no unnecessary noise

Walk 1
HIGH BARNET

*Oakwood — Hadley Common — Monken Hadley —
Barnet — Totteridge — Mill Hill East*

7½ miles   OS sheet 176

Barnet is on the London side of the GLC—Hertfordshire border
although local people prefer to claim to live in Hertfordshire as
in fact they once did. The Walk tends to be on high ground and
away from the Borough of Barnet's suburban housing. The
tube deposits the walker on the very edge of Trent Park and
there are useful Red Bus routes on both sides of the town. This
Walk can be divided — the first stage across Hadley Common
to Barnet tube is a rewarding 4 miles whilst the 3½ miles
between the two northern ends of the London Transport
Northern Line, High Barnet and Mill Hill East, offer a delightful village church and a well-defined country footpath.

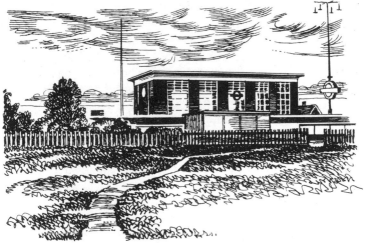

Oakwood Station

9

Oakwood Underground Station is the last but one stop on the Piccadilly Line and Mill Hill East Underground Station is on a branch line of the Northern Line.

Cross the main road outside Oakwood Station and enter Trent Park by the small entrance on one side of the railway bridge. A gravel footpath runs across grass to pass a pond (left) and enter a wood. The way is near the railway (left) and crosses the first of several streams which form part of the Merryhill Brook. The path then becomes enclosed and runs closer to the railway with a view to the east. When the gravel path bears half right beyond some bushes, keep forward along a faint path in the grass. The path dips to cross a stream. Beyond another field the way is through a hedge gap and over a further field and stream. On reaching a stream in a copse keep ahead over a plank footbridge whilst the railway swings away to Cockfosters.

TRENT PARK takes its name from Trent, South Tyrol where George III's doctor, Sir Richard Jebb, attended the Duke of Gloucester. The grateful King granted this estate to Jebb. The grounds, laid out by Humphry Repton with grass and woodland, are now a 360-acre GLC Country Park with nature and farm trails, a riding school and a 2¾-mile horse ride. The mansion, which is used as a college, was refaced in 1926 with bricks from the demolished Devonshire House which stood in Piccadilly opposite Green Park. In 1935 Sir Philip Sassoon lent the house for part of the late Duke and Duchess of Kent's honeymoon. Sassoon also brought the obelisk (on the Park's north side), which commemorates the birth of an earlier Duke of Kent's son, from Wrest Park in Bedfordshire. Camlet Moat, near the north gate, is featured in Sir Walter Scott's 'The Fortunes of Nigel' as the scene of Lord Dalgano's murder. Christ Church, Cockfosters, just to the west of the estate, was built in 1839 by Robert Bevan of Trent Park to save his servants having to walk into Enfield for services. Oakwood Station opened as Enfield West Station in 1933.

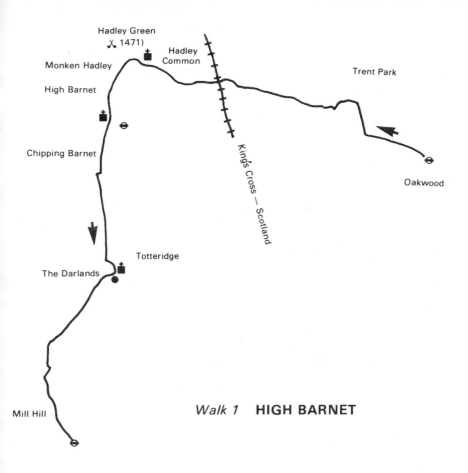

Hadley Green
X 1471)
Monken Hadley
Hadley Common
High Barnet
Trent Park
Chipping Barnet
Kings Cross — Scotland
Oakwood
Totteridge
The Darlands
Mill Hill

Walk 1 **HIGH BARNET**

Go forward up the gentle grass incline. There is a hedge to
the left and a view to the right across to the hills near Epping
Forest. Cross a wide footbridge and enter the wood ahead.
Follow the now gravel path which bends and runs ahead for a
few yards. At a junction do not go right on to the long wooded
path but turn left to cross a ditch and bear right on a narrow
path through trees and bushes. Cross a stream at the bottom
of the path and walk up the grass bank ahead. When the lodge
comes into view keep ahead towards the gateway by the
building. The metalled carriageway from the house is to the
right.

On reaching the lodge, go through the tall gateway and turn
right along the main road. After a short distance go left into

11

Chalk Lane. Just before The Cock (ahead) bear right into Games Road and pass through a white wooden gateway leading to Hadley Common.

The metalled lane follows the edge of the Common and soon the houses (left) end and the path becomes rough as it goes through the trees. Keep near the left boundary as the path runs gently downhill to cross a narrow bridge over a stream just below Beech Hill Lake (out of sight to the right).

A now gravel way runs ahead and briefly emerges into the open where there is a glimpse (half left) of Chipping Barnet Church (*see page 15*) on the hill. The way bends and becomes metalled before climbing through the trees up Baker Hill. Cross the railway bridge, over the King's Cross—Scotland line, and continue ahead through the trees.

On emerging into the open, the path again becomes a lane with occasional traffic. As the lane climbs Priddeon's Hill there is a parallel path in the trees (right). Beyond the Hadley Road gate (left) there are houses (left) and the trees (right) fall back from the road. In front of one of the houses (left) there is the Common's cattle pound. Next to the small entrance to King George's Playing Field is Hadley, an eleven-bedroom house designed by Sir Christopher Wren. Beyond Lemmons (behind the hedge, left) the road reaches a junction with Camlet

---

MONKEN HADLEY. 'Monken' recalls that the church belonged to the monks of Waldon in Essex whilst 'Hadley' means high place. The present church was erected in the 1490s and restored in 1850 by G. E. Street. The tower's beacon, still lit on special occasions, is an eighteenth-century successor to one which formed part of a chain at the time of the Spanish Armada threat. Lemmons, next to The Hermitage just inside the Common, was the home of writers Kingsley Amis and Elizabeth Jane Howard until 1975. Poet Laureate Cecil Day Lewis died here in 1972 shortly after completing his last poem 'At Lemmons'. The nine-bedroom eighteenth-century house is featured in Amis's novel *Girl 20* and the garden is described by Elizabeth Jane Howard in *Odd Girl Out*.

Cherub on convent wall at Monken Hadley

Way. Keep ahead to pass through Monken Hadley gate.

Keep to the left-hand pavement beyond the gateway and follow the road round a bend. Stay on the pavement where the road divides and pass the early seventeenth-century Wilbraham Almshouses (left). Keep by the houses and just near Livingstone Cottage cross the road to follow a parallel path along Hadley Green.

On reaching a pond (left), the path joins the end of Barnet High Street. Walk along the street to pass Ye Olde Monken Holt, a prize-winning pub (right).

Monken Hadley gate

13

Monken Hadley almshouses

Where the High Street bears left by the church, keep ahead up the narrow Church Passage to reach Wood Street. Cross the road and walk between buildings to the entrance to the Old Court Recreation Ground. There are toilets (right) just before the gateway.

Go ahead through the park and take the right-hand path where the way divides at flowerbeds. Go to the left of the bowling green and follow the path round the back of the green where the way turns sharply left to run south. The long enclosed path passes several tennis courts before meeting

HADLEY GREEN. The Battle of Barnet, the climax of the Wars of the Roses, was fought here on Easter Day 1471 when Warwick 'the Kingmaker' died along with over 1,000 others in the presence of Edward IV and the deposed Henry VI. A monument at **Hadley Highstone**, at the north end, marks the place (then in a wood) where Warwick died. David Livingstone (*see page 46*) lived at Livingstone Cottage for nine months in 1857 whilst on his first leave after 17 years in Africa. More recently James Agate, the drama critic, lived here. Lord Carr of Hadley lived two doors away at the eighteenth-century Monkenholt when he was Home Secretary in the early 1970s. The magnificent Hadley House is also eighteenth-century.

Hadley Green

CHIPPING BARNET. 'Chipping' refers to the market which is still held here on Wednesdays and Saturdays. The parish church of St John the Baptist is a fifteenth-century building which was restored by William Butterfield in 1875. Now that Barnet is a London borough this church is a rival to 'London's highest church' at Highgate (*see page 21*) since both are about the same level and higher than St Paul's Cathedral. General Monck stayed at The Mitre in 1660 when on his way from Scotland to London to prepare for the Restoration of Charles II. Samuel Pepys dined at The Red Lion on Barnet Hill in 1667 when he visited the Physic Well at the end of Wellhouse Lane. The Red Lion (now rebuilt but still displaying its lion high over the pavement) was a Tory meeting place whilst the Whigs gathered at The Green Man in the High Street where Peel and Palmerston stayed. The Barnet Museum in Wood Street is open Tuesdays and Thursdays from 2.30 to 4.30pm and Saturdays from 10.30am to 4.30pm, admission free. In the High Street there is a small branch of McDonald's, the hamburger chain, which is open daily.

Mays Lane. Cross the road to a row of shops and turn right. At a post box go left up Leeside. When the houses end the road meets a gate and swings to the left. Here, keep ahead on a metalled footpath across the grass and cross the footbridge over the Dollis Brook.

Follow the enclosed metalled footpath which runs between fields and then climbs a hill. Where the way passes between metal barriers there is a view back to Chipping Barnet Church. The path crosses the end of a road and continues between hedges. After crossing the top of an unmetalled lane the path passes under a wooden barrier and becomes a grassed way leading to a gate at Totteridge village.

Turn left to pass Lime Grove (left) and follow the road round a bend past the war memorial (left) to reach Totteridge Church.

Walk down the footpath which begins at gates between The Darlands and Garden Hill opposite the church. The enclosed path runs downhill, giving views over fields (right). At the bottom of the hill the path runs almost straight ahead along

TOTTERIDGE belonged to the Bishop of Ely in the thirteenth century. The church was built in 1790 but has a Jacobean pulpit. Cardinal Manning was born opposite in 1805 at Copped Hall (on the site of The Darlands) and, as an Anglican, attended the church. He received news of the Battle of Waterloo from an uncle and aunt who called here. Although the family moved to Kent just after 1815 he returned to attend school and visited the village when he was a Cardinal. His father and brother are buried on the east side of the churchyard. Sir Lucas Pepys, George III's doctor (*see page 82*), is buried to the south of the church. Lord Hewart, Lord Chief Justice during the inter-war years, was married here and lived in the eighteenth-century Garden Hill opposite; he is buried in an unmarked grave. Totteridge Ornamental Waters (to the south and privately owned) were created in the early nineteenth century after Cardinal Manning's mother had laid sheets on the ground to see where the lake would look best from the house.

the edge of a wood (left) for over ¼ mile. Beyond the wooden stile at the end go half left across an open field in the direction of the large National Institute for Medical Research building on the hill.

Cross a wooden stile in the far corner of the field and keep ahead at the path junction. The enclosed way runs between a stream (left) and a wooden fence to the entrance to Folly Farm's new farmhouse. Turn left to follow a lane along the side of a cricket ground (right). The road becomes enclosed and bears left to a junction with Burtonhole Lane.

Turn right up the hill and at the top, just beyond White Cottage (left), turn left into the unmetalled Eleanor Crescent. After just a few yards turn right to pass between wooden barriers and follow a (at first) narrow path through a wood. The path keeps near the edge of the wood and after ¼ mile reaches The Ridgeway at Mill Hill.

Turn left along the road. Red Bus 240 runs along here to Mill Hill East Station which is ahead at the bottom of Bittacy Hill.

MILL HILL. Nell Gwynne and Charles II are believed to have stayed at Littleberries, now part of St Vincent's Convent. The almshouses at the top of Milespit Hill are seventeenth-century. Mill Hill School was founded in 1807 as a 'grammar school for Protestant Dissenters' and here in 1870 Sir James Murray began work on *The Oxford English Dictionary* with help from the boys. More recent pupils include Kingsley Martin, Richard Dimbleby, Sir Norman Hartnell and Denis Thatcher. The path of Church Cottage was made over a hundred years ago with upturned inkpots, obtained from the school. St Paul's Church, next door, was built by William Wilberforce, the reformer, in the face of opposition from the Vicar of Hendon who enjoyed a private income from slave plantations. Cardinal Vaughan founded the famous Mill Hill Missionaries at the eighteenth-century Holcombe House at the west end of the village.

Walk 2
HAMPSTEAD AND HIGHGATE

Alexandra Palace — Highgate — Hampstead Heath — Hampstead

5¾ miles   OS sheet 176

Whilst the residents of Hampstead and Highgate fiercely guard their village life they are pleased to see visitors admiring the preserved buildings and using the local footpaths. Remarkably, part of this Walk is in the same London borough as Bloomsbury and Holborn.

British Rail trains run direct from Moorgate Underground Station (Circle and Northern Lines) and Finsbury Park (Piccadilly and Victoria Lines) to Alexandra Palace Station. The Northern Line serves Highgate and Hampstead where there are also, of course, Red Buses.

On leaving Alexandra Palace Station bear left to cross the railway by the pedestrian bridge. Turn left at the end and follow Bedford Road round a bend to Alexandra Park. Keep on the pavement which climbs up to pass the front of Alexandra Palace.

At the second road bend, on the far side of the Palace, cross the road and follow a path which leads towards an old railway bridge. Just before the bridge, turn left to follow a narrow path. There is a car park on the left. Keep to the path ahead and ignore all turnings. The way passes the Kids Own Kaff (open 12 noon to 6.00pm on Sundays, Bank Holidays and some Saturdays) which boasts Marine Ices and Sainsbury's tea on the menu.

The path soon runs through a covered way above Muswell Hill Primary School. Turn left at a T-junction to walk under Muswell Hill and emerge on the old Alexandra Palace— Highgate railway line. A now gravel path runs through the

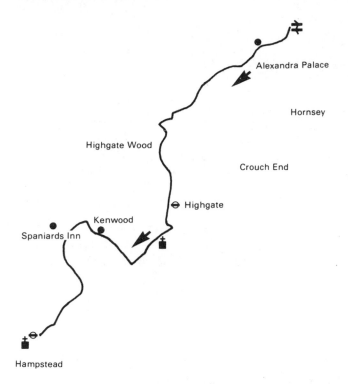

Walk 2 **HAMPSTEAD AND HIGHGATE**

ALEXANDRA PALACE is a famous landmark and a venue for concerts, meetings and exhibitions. The Park opened in 1863 when the Prince of Wales married Princess Alexandra of Denmark and ten years later the Palace was completed. However, the building had to be re-erected following a fire caused by a workman's brazier on the lead roof. After much controversy the Palace is again being restored following another devastating fire in 1980. From the beginning there was a railway branch line from Highgate to a station at the back of the Palace but the last passenger train ran in 1954 and the line has now become a footpath. The first regular television programmes were transmitted from this high point and BBC Television News was based here long after other BBC departments had moved to central London.

Alexandra Palace railway path

trees. There is a break in the woodland as the path crosses a viaduct affording unusual views over Hornsey and Crouch End. On passing under Muswell Hill Road the path becomes metalled and bears left to join the road. Cranley Gardens Station was situated on the west side of the bridge. Keep ahead for a few yards to go right, through the wooden gates of Highgate Wood.

Ignore the first turning and keep ahead on the metalled path. At a junction by a gateway (right), turn left on to another metalled path which runs deep into the wood. At a further junction by a drinking fountain (left), which bears some lines from local poet Coleridge, turn right. On approaching the back of a refreshment pavilion bear half left through the trees to take another metalled path which joins from the left. Continue on this path (which has a gravel surface for a short distance) to pass a playground (right) and go over a cross path. The woodland path leads to gates near the top of Muswell Hill Road.

Turn right to walk up the hill to the junction with Archway Road. Highgate Underground Station is to the right.

The Walk continues ahead up Southwood Lane to pass Well Cottage (a Bow Street Runners' house) on the corner of The

HIGHGATE refers to the gate which stood here at the entrance to the Bishop of London's park. St Michael's Church was built only in 1833 and is the highest church in London. Samuel Taylor Coleridge, who lived opposite at 33 The Grove, is buried in the nave near a memorial to his landlord, Dr James Gillman. The east window is by Evie Hone whose work can also be seen at Downe (*see page 64*). Peter Bowles, the actor, was married here. The Flask dates from the seventeenth century and has associations with Dick Turpin, who hid in the cellar, and Hogarth who instantly sketched a distorted face after a customer had been hit during a quarrel. Another pub, The Wrestlers in North Road, maintains the 300-year-old ceremony of 'swearing on the horns', which recalls the time when Highgate was an overnight stop for men driving live cattle to Smithfield. A. E. Housman wrote 'A Shropshire Lad' at nearby Byron Cottage during the 1890s. Highgate School was founded during Elizabeth I's reign and used to dominate village life. Past pupils include poets Gerard Manley Hopkins and John Betjeman and British Foreign Secretary Anthony Crosland.

Peter Sellers attended St Aloysius College in Hornsey Lane near St Joseph's (or Holy Joe's) on Highgate Hill. At the bottom of the hill (near Archway Underground Station) there is the Whittington Stone marking the spot where Dick Whittington and his cat heard the bells calling 'Turn again, Whittington'. Less than half-way down the hill there is Lauderdale House, dating from the Tudor period and named after Lady Lauderdale who inherited the house in 1645. After Charles I's execution she was forced to hand over the building to Cromwell's relation John Ireton. At the Restoration she reclaimed her property and Ireton seems to have moved across the road to where Ireton House now stands. In 1669 Lord Lauderdale moved to Ham House (*see page 105*) and Lauderdale House was let to Nell Gwynne who was looking after her royal baby. John Wesley preached here in 1782 and described the house as 'one of the most elegant boarding houses in England'. Refreshments are available in the house daily except for Mondays, 10.30am to 5.00pm.

Muswell Hill

Park (right). Later the road passes explorer Mary Kingsley's childhood home (left; number 22) and runs between the buildings of Highgate School in Highgate village.

Turn left along Highgate High Street and then right into South Grove to pass Pond Square (right) and then reach St Michael's Church (left) and The Flask (right). Continue ahead past the entrance to Witanhurst (right) and down Highgate West Hill.

HIGHGATE WEST HILL. The 65-room Witanhurst mansion was rebuilt in 1913 by Sir Arthur Crosfield, the Liberal MP. Below the house, on the site of number 40, stood The Fox where Queen Victoria rested after the landlord had halted a bolting horse pulling the royal carriage. The Queen, in only the second week of her reign, granted The Fox (which soon became The Fox & Crown) the right to display the Royal Arms. Further down the hill is number 31 where Betjeman lived as a child and saw sheep being driven up the hill. He recalls the house in *Summoned by Bells* and described the view as his 'first memory of countryside'.

Coleridge's home at Highgate

Beyond the bend turn right down Merton Lane to reach Millfield Lane on the edge of Hampstead Heath.

Do not turn sharp right into Fitzroy Park but go right (ignoring the 'Access only to residents' notice) to follow the un-metalled section of Millfield Lane. Later the metalled surface is resumed but where the way becomes rough again turn left through iron gates to follow a parallel metalled path to Kenwood House.

Walk along the terrace in front of the house (right) and continue through the Lime Walk. Just beyond the Lime Walk

---

MILLFIELD LANE was probably once a farm track. Leigh Hunt referred to it as 'Poets Lane' and certainly it was known to Keats who on different occasions met Hunt, Coleridge and Hazlitt here. Dr Edith Summerskill, the anti-boxing campaigner who became Baroness Summerskill of Ken Wood, lived at Pond House (at the south-eastern end). The lane passes the Ladies' Bathing Pond where Margaret Rutherford, the actress, used to swim every morning.

Kenwood House

turn right at a path junction and then at once go left on to a well-worn path which curves across the Heath. On reaching an iron gateway (where there is a view back to Kenwood) go through the gateway and turn left up a wide path which soon opens out over the brow of the hill. Pass under an oak tree and bear half right along a narrower woodland path. On reaching a cross path, turn right to walk along another lime avenue known as The Boundary Path. After just over ¼ mile the path meets a road.

KENWOOD. The present building dates from 1694. Lord Mansfield, the Lord Chief Justice, bought the brick house in 1754 and ten years later called in Robert Adam to remodel the country house and add the Orangery and Library. Kenwood remained a country retreat *until 1780* when Mansfield's Bloomsbury home was burnt by the Gordon rioters who, having enjoyed the contents of the cellar there, made their way here to destroy Kenwood — Hampstead Lane then passed the front door. Fortunately the landlord of the nearby Spaniards Inn plied the men with wine until the military arrived. Kenwood then became the family's permanent home. Mansfield's son later added the two wings and moved the road away from the house. The family eventually sold the property in 1925 and Lord Iveagh, the purchaser, gave Kenwood to the nation. The art treasures inside include works by Romney, who lived in Hampstead; Vermeer's 'Guitar Player', stolen in 1974 but safely returned; Gainsborough's 'Greyhounds Coursing a Fox', which came from Mentmore, and his 'Pink Lady'. The house is open daily from 10.00am to dusk; admission is free. There is a café on the east side. The wood itself is the remains of the Middlesex Forest and the sweeping lawn is the setting for the famous open air concerts. Below the Lime Walk can be seen the source of the River Fleet which still flows under the end of Fleet Street. Peeping out of the bushes north of the Lime Walk is the thatched summerhouse used by Dr Johnson in Streatham between 1766 and 1782 (*see page 66*).

Cross the main road to walk along Well Walk. There are seats on the corner where Keats used to sit looking at the Heath. Keep to the high pavement on the right to pass the site of the Hampstead Wells near number 13 (right) where Henry Hyndman, founder of the Social Democratic Federation, lived and died. Number 40 (left) is John Constable's last home. Further ahead on the right is Burgh House which is open for tea (Wednesdays to Sundays) until 5.30pm.

Beyond Burgh House follow Flask Walk to Hampstead High Street. Turn right for Hampstead Underground Station.

Constable's Well Walk house

26

HAMPSTEAD, built on the side of a hill, became fashionable in the early eighteenth century when spa water was discovered in Well Walk. One of the first writers to visit Hampstead was Dr Johnson who came here in 1745 to stay just behind the then new parish church of St John. Constable's tomb can be found in the churchyard. Across the road are interred the remains of actress Kay Kendall and Labour leader Hugh Gaitskell. At the top of nearby Holly Walk is St Mary's Catholic Church, founded in 1796, where the exiled General de Gaulle worshipped and, more recently, actress Judi Dench and actor-writer Michael Williams were married. Sir William Walton once lived in the first cottage in Holly Berry Lane. St John's, Downshire Hill, is a private chapel whose congregation pay £1 a year rent to the owners; they are served by a chaplain, the first one having been a friend of Byron. Downshire Hill has associations with Rossetti who spent his honeymoon here, Bernard Shaw, D. H. Lawrence, Stanley Spencer, Katherine Mansfield, Flora Robson and Edith Sitwell. Keats watched the houses in this road being built from the windows of his cottage in Keats Grove (open daily; admission free). George Eliot worshipped regularly at the Rosslyn Hill Chapel nearby.

Walk 3
THE LEE VALLEY

Rye House — Broxbourne — Waltham Abbey

7 miles   OS sheet 166

The Lee Valley Park, estabished only in 1967, stretches over 20 miles from London's East End into Hertfordshire, the derelict land on each side of the River Lee having been restored to peaceful water meadows. The river was the only route open to carry essential supplies into the City of London during the Great Plague of 1665. This Walk comes south with the River Lee and the man-made New River from historic Rye House and

---

RYE HOUSE. Only the fifteenth-century gatehouse and moat remain. This was the scene of the alleged Rye House Plot in 1683 when the owner, Richard Rumbold, was said to be involved in a scheme to assassinate Charles II as he rode along the lane from Newmarket. The King changed his plan but the plot was 'disclosed' and Algernon Sidney, a former Cromwellian, and Lord William Russell were executed whilst part of Rumbold's body was said to have been pinned to his house. As a result of these convictions known Whig supporters were removed from office by the Tories. The gateway, which has an inset brick handrail on the spiral staircase and an exhibition devoted to the Plot, is open on summer weekends; admission is free. The nature reserve, managed by the Royal Society for the Protection of Birds, is also open at weekends from 10.00am to 5.00pm; admission is free. Vehicles on the toll road were once charged ½d a wheel to pass. The seventeenth-century Rye House pub, across the road, retains its very large bow windows.

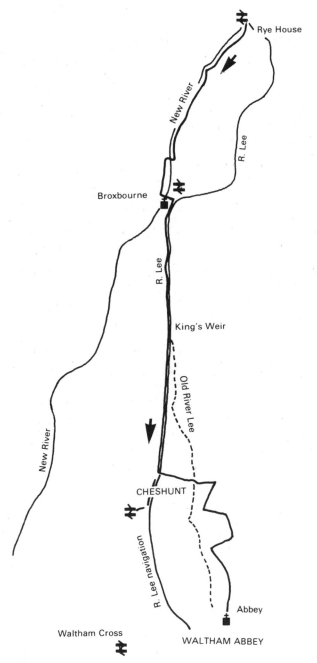

Rye House

New River

R. Lee

Broxbourne

R. Lee

King's Weir

Old River Lee

New River

CHESHUNT

R. Lee navigation

Abbey

Waltham Cross

WALTHAM ABBEY

Walk 3 **THE LEE VALLEY**

passes over fields to the Norman Waltham Abbey.

The valley is well served by British Rail's Liverpool Street–
Hertford line. There are stations at Rye House and Waltham
Cross. The Walk also passes Broxbourne Station and goes near
Cheshunt Station.

Rye House Station lies between the New River and the River
Lee. On leaving the station go right to see Rye House; otherwise go left to start the Walk at an iron kissing gate leading to
a path by the New River.

Soon the path bears left and then right over a stile – however, walkers do tend to cut the corner by continuing over the
iron fence to keep on the very edge of the water.

Beyond a footbridge (right) the way continues ahead along
an iron fence to the left and then right. The river soon bears
right to pass under a road. Pass through the iron kissing gates
which guard the road and continue to follow the water to pass
Hoddesdon Pumping Station (left). After another kissing gate
the short gravel path gives way to a grass surface. There is a
further kissing gate.

Pass through the iron kissing gates at Conduit Lane East.
Soon there is a deep drop (left) and a fine view across the Lee
Valley. After passing two footbridges (right) the way passes
through more iron kissing gates at a metalled road. There is
then one further footbridge (right) before the path reaches a
single kissing gate at a narrow lane. Here the New River continues ahead without a path whilst the Walk turns right over
the water.

NEW RIVER, cut during 1609–13, was once the source of
London's only pure water supply. The idea of bringing
water from Hertfordshire springs and the clean end of the
River Lee was pioneered by Sir Hugh Myddleton who had
made a fortune in the New World and enjoyed smoking
with Sir Walter Raleigh. There was strong opposition from
landowners to the plan but James I, who fell into the water
during an inspection, gave his support. The water flows
towards New River Head in Clerkenwell which is now the
headquarters of the Thames Water Authority.

River Lee at Broxbourne

Where the way divides by Albury Lodge (left) keep left on a rough path to reach a road junction. Keep left to bear left into St Catherine's Road and at the end of the road turn left into Churchfields. Soon there is a view of Broxbourne Church at the far end of the road.

Turn left at the crossroads before the church to pass The Kingfisher (left) and cross the New River. Broxbourne Station is to the left. At once bear half right to leave the main road and pass the Welcome Café (right). Follow the slope downhill and at the railway line turn right along a narrow rough path which leads down below the line. Cross a wooden footbridge over a stream and turn right to follow the water (right).

A worn path runs through the grass to a concrete bridge. Keep ahead on a metalled surface to pass a toilet block (left)

BROXBOURNE. St Augustine's, now on the banks of the New River, dates from about 1450 but has a Norman font. On the south aisle wall there is a memorial to John Loudon McAdam, 'the great improver of the British roads' who lived in nearby Hoddesdon from 1825 to 1836. To the north of the altar there is a Sheffington tomb displaying the family crest — a mermaid looking at herself in a mirror.

and bear right over the water by the remains of a mill. Turn left to follow the water (left) and pass a café (right). Walk under the railway line to meet the River Lee.

Turn right to follow the towpath with the river on the left. After ½ mile the gardens across the water give way to meadows and the towpath narrows. At King's Weir, where the old River Lee flows away to the left, the path keeps by the navigable section to pass under a bridge. After Turnford Marsh Lock the towpath narrows and enjoys various surfaces as it continues south to the next lock 1 mile away. On the way the towpath passes under a now disused footbridge at Holyfield Marsh — there was once a Benedictine nunnery to the west. Some 300 yards beyond Cheshunt Lock the path reaches a bridge.

To reach Cheshunt Station, ½ mile away, continue ahead along the canal and where the lake (right) ends turn right to walk through a car park. Beyond the toilets (right) a lane leads to a level crossing and the station.

Cornmill Stream at Waltham Abbey

Waltham Abbey gateway

The Walk continues over the metalled bridge which crosses the water. Bear half right into the trees and bushes to follow a narrow path. Soon there is a glimpse of water (right). Cross an iron footbridge over Hooksmarsh Ditch and follow an enclosed footpath. There are more glimpses of water (left and then right) and a high footbridge ahead. The path continues over the footbridge spanning a wide lake. The still-enclosed path runs gently down to a car park.

Cross the metalled car park and a bridge over the old River Lee, and bear left with the lane to pass Fisher's Green Farm. On reaching Fisher's Green Cottage (left) turn right to go over a stile. Follow the edge of the large field (right) to join a stream and then bear eastwards along a high wire fence (right). Turn right at the end of the fence. (A pink house can be seen to the east.) Pass the Ministry of Defence entrance (right) and follow the high wire fence (right) for 100 yards to cross a shallow ditch and enter a grassed area. Continue to follow the wire fence and turn right with the fence to reach a footbridge spanning Cornmill Stream. Cross the bridge and turn left to follow the water (left). Ahead is Waltham Abbey. After crossing three wooden stiles bear half right towards another

WALTHAM ABBEY. Waltham means 'weald homestead' and the small town is sometimes called Waltham Holy Cross after the miraculous crucifix brought here by King Canute's standard bearer. The church erected to house the cross was rebuilt by King Harold in 1060 after he experienced a cure whilst kneeling by the cross. He prayed here again on his way to the Battle of Hastings and is believed to be buried beyond the east end. Part of Henry II's penance for St Thomas à Becket's murder was the re-foundation of the religious community here as an Augustinian abbey. The monastery treasures included St Patrick's dalmatic. Henry III came for a religious retreat and Richard II stayed at the Abbey for a while during the Peasants' Revolt. Earlier, the body of Queen Eleanor had rested here as the nearby Waltham Cross (the last before Charing Cross) indicates. In 1529 the future Archbishop Cranmer was staying in the town when Henry VIII, desiring a divorce from Catherine of Aragon, was also visiting here. Waltham was the last monastery to be dissolved and among those displaced was the organist, Thomas Tallis, who found a temporary post at Canterbury. Most of the buildings, including part of the church, were destroyed; the old Norman nave remains as a parish church. (The east end now has windows by Burne-Jones.) The Vicarage was built in 1637 and an early incumbent was Thomas Fuller who had been chaplain to Charles I's daughter, Henrietta. The Abbey's bells inspired Tennyson's 'Ring Out Wild Bells' and it was here that the words 'Hark, the Herald Angels Sing' were first set to the familiar Mendelssohn tune. Refreshment is still available within the Abbey precinct — Lichgate House, built in 1600, is now a café (open daily 10.00am until, usually, after 6.00pm). The Epping Forest District Museum (open Friday to Monday, 2.00 to 5.00pm and Tuesdays 12 noon to 5.00pm; admission free) in Sun Street serves refreshments and has a new arbour commemorating the birth of Prince William of Wales.

Waltham Abbey

wooden stile below the by-pass. The dried-up Abbey fishponds are to the right.

Cross the stile and walk under the road. Bear half right across the grass to go over a stile by a white gate. Follow a rough track which becomes metalled by the Abbey gatehouse (left) before reaching the church's west door.

A signpost near the Abbey's west door points towards Waltham Cross Station 1 mile along High Bridge Street. Red Buses 217B, 242 and 250 pass the station.

King Harold's tomb

Walk 4
EPPING FOREST
Epping — Epping Forest — Loughton

5¾ miles   OS sheet 167

'London's Larder', the docks, may have disappeared but 'London's Back Garden' remains as safe as when Queen Victoria visited Epping Forest in 1882 and announced 'It gives me the greatest satisfaction to dedicate this beautiful forest for the use and enjoyment of my people for all time'. Even the persistent M25 has been forced under rather than through the north end of the Forest. The 6,000 acres, once part of the Royal Forest of Essex, were purchased in 1878 by the City of London to safeguard the area from development. More than half of the land is still woodland; there are 150 ponds and at least 144 different bird species, while the 100-strong herd of black fallow deer (actually dark brown) is believed to be the oldest in the country. Local residents still enjoy commoners' ancient grazing rights. This 12-mile crescent of trees and grass was often the first and only experience of countryside for East End children who would come here in huge numbers on Bank Holidays. Pearly kings and queens were once familiar figures at Chingford where there is a sixteenth-century hunting lodge. Dick Turpin, Alfred Lord Tennyson, William Morris, T. E. Lawrence and Jacob Epstein have all lived on the edge of the Forest. The Queen appoints the Ranger (at present the Duke of Gloucester), and the City administers the area — the familiar City of London shield can be seen on noticeboards. Forest maps are notoriously inaccurate but this Walk provides a taste of London's very own rural heritage on clear paths.

Epping and Loughton Stations are both on the London Transport Central Line and trains run direct to these stations from West London and Oxford Circus.

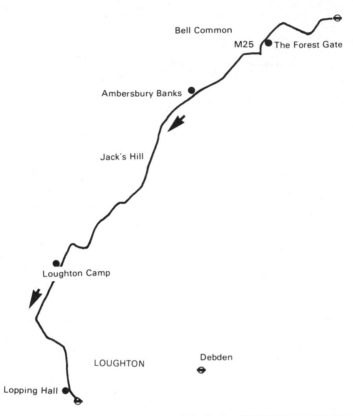

Walk 4 **EPPING FOREST**

Turn right out of Epping Station and after a few yards turn left to go between the car park and a hut. The enclosed way later turns left with the car park (left) before turning right up a flight of steps. Turn left at a road (Centre Drive) and ignore turnings until you pass The Crescent (right), then go right up Western Avenue where there is an expanse of grass and a seat under a solitary tree. The road bears left behind the tree. Where there is a view of fields ahead do not go downhill but turn right on to a footpath next to number 29.

The narrow footpath runs ahead between bushes. Where the main path turns sharply right, go round the left side of the

Pathway through Epping Forest

EPPING means 'forest clearing' and was an important stop on the main road to London. St John's Church, designed by G. F. Bodley (*see page 128*), was built in 1889 when All Saints, Epping Upland, ceased to be the parish church. St John's was originally the site of a Norman chapel served by monks from Waltham Abbey (*see page 34*). John Overall, vicar of Epping in the early 1590s, helped to translate the Authorised Version of the Bible under James 1. The United Reformed Church in Lindsey Road was founded during James I's reign and claims to be one of the oldest local free churches in the country, although its eighteenth-century building has been greatly modernised. Charles II, William III and Queen Anne all visited the town when being entertained at nearby Copped Hall (to the west). Samuel Pepys paid a visit in 1660. Henry Doubleday, the nineteenth-century Quaker naturalist, lived on the corner of Buttercross Lane (the Buttercross was removed in 1781). Winston Churchill was Member of Parliament for Epping during his wartime premiership. The weekly Monday market succeeded the Friday market begun in 1575 under Elizabeth I.

bushes ahead to find the path continuing forward. (Many walkers appear to take a parallel path further left which runs below the public footpath.) Our path runs into the open to follow the left side of a field very gently uphill. The way runs through a gap to a concrete signpost.

Bear half left across a metalled road to follow a line of houses (left) along Bell Common. The path surface improves to become metalled and meets Theydon Road by The Forest Gate (left).

The Walk continues ahead on a new road (over the unseen M25). Before the road passes Bowlands Meadow (left) or Warreners (right) turn right up a rough track called Forest Ride. Where the main track bears left keep going ahead. The wooded path then narrows and emerges in a clearing at the top of a long forest ride.

Go between the logs to walk along the wide forest clearing. The path is grassed but used by horses and liable to be muddy. Later, where a path joins from the left the way enjoys a firmer surface. The path dips and rises and at one point runs very close to Ambersbury Banks. The earthworks can be seen (right) in the trees soon after one of the dips in the path.

THE FOREST GATE pub dates from at least the sixteenth century and is still a free house. Regular customers here were drovers who walked bullocks through the town to Smithfield in London. Although efforts had been made to stop Londoners crossing the River Lee during the 1665 Great Plague, the disease spread to Epping and supplies for the town were delivered to a point outside the inn. The Bell Common Post Office opposite sells food and is open on Sunday mornings.

AMBERSBURY BANKS is an early Iron Age earthwork thrown up between 300BC and AD10. It is said to have been Queen Boadicea's base in AD43 when she set out to make her final stand against the Roman general Suetonius Paulinus who slew 80,000 Britons.

Epping Forest

The bridleway soon reaches the Theydon Bois road (itself just a bridleway in the nineteenth century) at Jack's Hill. Cross the road to follow the woodland gravel path ahead known as The Ditches. After less than ½ mile, before the path runs steeply downhill, turn right on to a less-well-defined path.

Bindweed

Sweet chestnuts

The way soon bears left and as the path begins to run downhill there is a good gravel surface. Beyond a stream the path climbs steeply and, after a double bend, reaches a main road known as Goldings Hill. Here there are bus stops for Red Bus 201 linking Epping and Loughton.

Cross the road to continue on the wide way — the Forest's Green Ride. The gravel path withstands the regular traffic of horses well, leaving a good walking surface. The way bends and runs up and downhill. After crossing two streams the path runs steeply uphill and bears right. Where it narrows there is a view (right) down into a small wooded valley. Then the path turns steeply south and after ¼ mile crosses a path known as Clay Road — here there are two seats made from logs. This was the part of the Forest known to Jacob Epstein who lived and worked on his sculptures ½ mile to the east on Baldwin's Hill.

The Walk continues ahead to pass near (right) Loughton camp, another earthwork but less distinct than Ambersbury Banks. The path runs downhill and over a stream. Beyond the stream the way climbs gently. Some 300 yards farther on, after a steeper climb, leave the gravel path by bearing half left on to a less-used path. The (sometimes narrow) path runs through trees and bushes to reach a road junction on the edge of Loughton. Turn left across the top of Staples Road to follow

LOUGHTON. Between 1856 and 1865 Loughton village was at the end of the railway line. The struggle to preserve the Forest was centred here just as the line was being extended to Epping. In 1865 the Rev John Maitland, who was both a landowner and the Rector of Loughton, fenced off 1,300 acres of the Forest to sell as building plots. Tom Willingale, a 73-year-old forester objected and found himself evicted from his cottage on 9th November. Two days later he took part in the annual ceremony on nearby Staples Hill where villagers confirmed their ancient right to cut firewood. At midnight on 10th November a fire was lit on the hill and Lopping Day began with firewood being ritually cut. The following year the landowners offered a free dinner to foresters at The King's Head on the evening of 10th November. Willingale accepted the generous hospitality but stayed sober enough to be able to slip out just before midnight and perform the Lopping Day ceremony and return brandishing a newly cut branch at his horrified hosts. Villagers continued to ignore the fences although the landlords attempted court proceedings. When members of Willingale's family were prosecuted he brought a lawsuit. He died before the case was completed but the City figures who had advised the old forester persuaded the City Corporation (which had already bought land for a cemetery at Manor Park) to come to the rescue of the village and save the Forest for all Londoners. The Epping Forest Act was passed in 1878 and Loughton's Lopping Hall was built with part of the £7,000 paid to the village by the City for the Lopping Rights. Villagers in the act of lopping are depicted above the Hall's doorway in Station Road. St Mary's, in the High Road, was built during the dispute. The old village church, rebuilt in the late 1870s, is near Debden Station. Sarah Martin, who wrote 'Old Mother Hubbard', is buried on the east side of the old churchyard. Trap's Hill, off the High Road, is reputed to be haunted by Dick Turpin who drags a woman behind his horse.

Forest Road into the town. (Walkers who miss the final forest path should turn left at the main road to follow the road into Loughton.)

Keep ahead to pass The Royal Oak (right) and its neighbour The Victoria Tavern. Go across Loughton's main shopping street and pass (right) Lopping Hall in Station Road. Loughton Station lies at the end of the road.

Lopping Hall at Loughton

Walk 5
ONGAR

Ongar — Greensted — North Weald Bassett

4½ miles   OS sheet 167

The Walk begins at the end of the London Transport Central Line at Ongar Station and follows part of the 50-mile Denham — Epping Essex Way towards North Weald Station where open countryside runs right up to the platform. Beyond Epping Station, the final six miles of the Central Line is a single track running through fields and woods. The line was laid in 1865 and remained steam operated until 1957. Blake Hall Station was only being used by seven regular passengers when it closed in 1981. A few years earlier a rabbit had jumped on to a train and bitten the driver. Now trains only run beyond Epping during the weekday peak periods and Red Bus 201 links Epping, North Weald and Ongar Stations all day and during weekends. (The last Ongar train out of Epping on a weekday morning leaves just before 9.00 and the first after-noon train is about 3.45. Remember to change on to the shorter train at Epping.) Walkers using the 201 bus should alight either at Ongar Station bus stop or in the village centre just before the last stop. This is a very rural walk and on Sundays there is no café and little pub food. Greensted churchyard has several seats and is the best spot for a picnic.

On leaving Ongar Station walk up to the main road and turn right to reach the village centre. Turn right at The Cock to walk down Banson's Lane at the side of The Taste Bud Café. At the bottom of the hill the lane crosses the Cripsey Brook. Do not bear left but keep ahead on the footpath which runs ahead for ½ mile. The way climbs gently and soon there is a view (right) of the white Blake Hall which gave its name to the now closed station between North Weald and Ongar. Ahead in

45

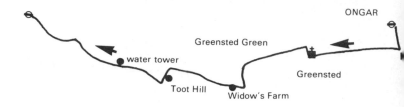

ONGAR

Greensted Green

water tower

Greensted

Toot Hill

Widow's Farm

Walk 5 **ONGAR**

the distance can be seen the front door of Greensted Hall.
On reaching a wooden stile keep ahead over the metalled
drive. Go through the wooden kissing gate and keep near the
wooden fence (right) to go through the gap (where there is
sometimes a gate) at the far end of the field. Keep forward
towards two trees at the end of a second field. After passing a
pond (left) go through a kissing gate under the left-hand tree.

ONGAR. Sir John Betjeman expressed an interest in
becoming stationmaster here. The village's full name is
Chipping Ongar indicating that Ongar (a hill) was once a
market town. The castle which stood at the end of Castle
Street was built by one of Henry II's knights who was
involved in Thomas à Becket's murder. The King visited
the new castle in 1157. King John came before Magna
Carta and Elizabeth I passed through in 1579 at about the
time the castle was demolished. The Norman church was
restored in 1884. Oliver Cromwell's niece, Jane Pallavicini,
is buried at the south end of the altar and the tomb of
Edward Boodle, who founded Boodle's in St James's, is
outside the south wall. The United Reformed Church was
built in 1833 and known to David Livingstone who lived in
the room over the archway. There he wrote to the London
Missionary Society asking if he could go to Africa. Jane
Taylor, who wrote 'Twinkle, Twinkle Little Star', is buried
in the chapel's vestry. The Taste Bud, the community
centre café, is open Tuesdays to Saturdays 9.30am to
2.00pm (5.00pm Saturdays).

Livingstone's room

Ongar-Greensted path

Walk ahead up the metalled drive and turn right to find the entrance to Greensted Church.

The Walk continues past the church (right) and through the gateway of Hall Farm. Keep between the farm buildings to near the bottom of the hill. Just before reaching an iron gate on the left, turn left over a sleeper footbridge to enter a field. Keep ahead alongside a hedge (right). The way continues over a stream into a second field and on approaching a third field crosses a tiny wooden footbridge and a stile. Keep ahead to pass the edge of Greensted Wood (right) and reach a road. Turn left for a few yards and then go right by a footpath sign to enter a field and walk up the side of a wood (left). When the wood ends there is a glimpse of new houses. Just before the wood resumes turn left through a very narrow gap in the hedge to pass a mound (left). Bear right to pass stables (left) and the wood (right). Keep forward along the side of a field to go through a gap at the far end.

Turn right to pass Widow's Farm (left) and keep to the left of the field boundary beyond the large gap (right). (From this high path there are clear views through the hedge to Greensted Green where the Tolpuddle Martyrs lived. In the centre of the

---

GREENSTED—JUXTA—ONGAR. The Saxon church is the world's oldest log church. The chancel arch is Norman and the tower is fourteenth-century. The priest's door was added during the Tudor period when tiles first replaced the thatched roof. The body of St Edmund, martyred in 870, rested here in 1013 on its way to Bury St Edmunds. James Brine, one of the Tolpuddle Martyrs, married the daughter of fellow martyr Thomas Stanfield here in 1839 after the pardoned farmworkers had come to Essex to escape any lingering prejudice in Dorset. The church was featured on the 3p stamp in 1972 when the rector was John Garrington, husband of the Rev Elsie Chamberlain. A herb festival is held here every two years and dried herbs are always on sale at the Rectory which also offers overnight accommodation to walkers (Tel: Ongar 364694).

mainly white houses can be seen the black wooden barn where they hosted Chartist meetings.) After ¼ mile the path passes an isolated concrete footpath sign indicating the little-used footpath to Greensted Green. Keep forward to reach the corner of this huge field. The path runs steeply down a bank and climbs more gently up to the next field — it may still be necessary to stoop to avoid a leaning tree. Continue westwards along the edge of the field (right) and cross a footbridge into another field where the way becomes enclosed.

On approaching Weald Farm take the right fork when the path divides at a large blackberry bush. Cross the footbridge over a stream where there is a good view (to the east) back towards Ongar. Turn left to continue westwards for a short distance to find a wooden stile on the left. Cross the stile and go ahead past Weald Farm Cottage and Weald Lodge to join a road at a bend. Keep forward on the road to Toot Hill.

Just before a green and The Green Man (right) turn right up a narrow metalled lane. There are high hedges on each side and after ¼ mile the lane reaches Clunes House (left) and a water tower.

Greensted Church

Buffers

Continue straight ahead past the water tower and a barn
(right) whilst the Essex Way continues half left towards
Epping. The footpath follows a hedge (left) along the side of a
large field to a wood ahead. On reaching the trees the path
bends slightly to follow the edge of the wood (right). Where the
track divides bear right through the middle of a second wood.
Soon after passing a large pond (right) the path leaves the
wood and follows the right-hand side of a field. Over to the
right are the masts of British Telecom's Ongar Radio Station.
The path enters a second field at a gap. North Weald Station
can be seen half left below.

Do not climb over the ladderstile but turn left to follow the
two sides of a field to Cold Hall Farm. Go round the farm

NORTH WEALD BASSETT. 'Weald' means 'forest' and
the Bassett family were lords of the manor in the thirteenth century. The church, which lies ¾ mile to the north
of the village, has an early Tudor brick tower. The airfield
was a fighter base during the Battle of Britain and there
are memorials to the dead pilots in the churchyard. The
King's Head, a coaching inn, is Tudor.

buildings to the farm entrance and turn right on to the farm's main track. Where the way bends left keep ahead and follow a hedge (left) to the level crossing at North Weald Station. To reach the 201 bus stop (outside The King's Head), walk down to the main road and turn right.

North Weald level crossing

Walk 6
THE DARENTH VALLEY

Swanley — Eynsford — Lullingstone —
Shoreham — Otford

7 miles   OS sheets 177 & 188

Arthur Mee lived on the side of the Darenth Valley and described the Kentish view as 'unique on the map of rural England'. More than a hundred years earlier the artist Samuel Palmer called the area 'the veil of heaven'. He said that Shoreham was so near London that Shoreham hops were cheaper in Southwark's Borough Market than in the village. Londoners continued to come here for hop picking until the mid 1950s.

The Walk begins at the end of Red Bus route 21A. British Rail's Swanley—Sevenoaks railway line runs parallel to the Walk and provides useful stations at Eynsford and Shoreham as well as Otford. Swanley can be reached from both Blackfriars Station (except weekends) and Victoria Station.

On arriving at Swanley bus garage, at the end of the High Street, cross the road and continue to walk in a south-easterly direction out of Swanley, leaving the garage on the left. Follow the pavement as it bears right over a dual carriageway. Cross the top of a lane and pass a row of houses (right). Continue ahead round the edge of a huge roundabout and down the road ahead. On the left side there is a long garage with yellow doors.

On coming level with a pylon (right) leave the traffic and turn on to a parallel road which runs behind a bank and soon loses its metalled surface. The way becomes narrow and the bank (left) falls away at the entrance to Pedham Place. Turn right on to a long concrete path. Before reaching the two warehouses (left) turn left off the concrete path to follow a wire fence (right) which soon bears right along the back of farm

52

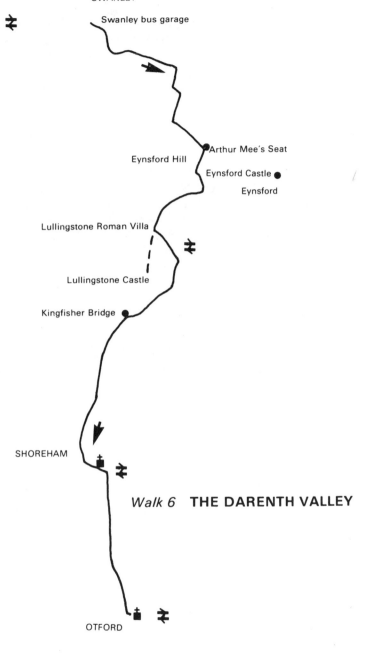

SWANLEY

Swanley bus garage

Arthur Mee's Seat

Eynsford Hill

Eynsford Castle

Eynsford

Lullingstone Roman Villa

Lullingstone Castle

Kingfisher Bridge

SHOREHAM

Walk 6 **THE DARENTH VALLEY**

OTFORD

buildings. As the way runs by a bank (right) there is a fine view ahead down the valley. The path turns sharply left and runs unfenced towards a wood. A straight narrow path runs just inside the wood to a viewpoint on Eynsford Hill.

Turn right over a stile to follow an enclosed path along the side of the hill. The way runs gently downhill to cross the metalled driveway to Arthur Mee's home. Continue ahead through a group of trees to follow a hedge and fence (right) down to another metalled drive. Follow this drive down to a lane and turn left.

EYNSFORD HILL. The present seat replaces one given in 1930 by Arthur Mee, editor of *The Children's Newspaper* and author of *The King's England*. In 1914 Mee had a house built nearby on the hill and described the view from here as 'a straight mile probably unique on the map of rural England'. He added, 'Roman, Norman, Saxon, Tudor — it is all in line, and in sight from Eynsford Hill'. Eynsford Castle (see below) can be seen in the valley and to the north there is the fifteenth-century tower of Farningham Church.

EYNSFORD. The church has a thirteenth-century tower but retains its Norman influence. When Thomas à Becket appointed a new incumbent to this parish, against the wishes of Sir William de Eynsford, the fatal breach with Henry II widened as William successfully appealed to the King. The ruins of William's Norman castle are open daily 9.30am to 6.30pm (4.00pm October to March); admission 30p, children and pensioners 15p. The sixteenth-century bridge by the ford was used as a pulpit by John Wesley. A pre-World War Two plan to replace the crossing with a new bridge was scrapped following the personal intervention of Transport Minister Hore-Belisha. Graham Sutherland, the artist, lived at Willow Cottage (opposite The Malt Shovel) in the early 1930s. The tearoom by the bridge is open daily until 5.00pm.

Eynsford Bridge and ford

On reaching The Cottage (right) leave the road to follow a narrow hedged footpath down to Sparepenny Lane. Turn right to a T-junction opposite Toll Bar Cottage in Eynsford.

Turn right at Toll Bar Cottage into Lullingstone Lane and

ROMAN VILLA. The mosaic floor was discovered in the mid-eighteenth century when a fence was being erected. The clay hill behind the building had slowly crept down to preserve the structure which was not excavated until 1949. The house dates from about AD80 and in the third century it appears to have been empty for about 50 years. New occupants then restored the house and created a mosaic floor. Later, but still 200 years before St Augustine's mission, a room was turned into a chapel for Christian worship. The residence was eventually abandoned after a fire early in the fifth century. It is open daily from 9.30am (2.00pm on Sundays) to 6.30pm (4.00pm October to March); admission 90p (50p in winter), children and pensioners 50p and 25p.

---

follow the road round a bend. There are usually some highland cattle in the long field under the viaduct. Continue along the lane to reach Lullingstone Roman Villa.

Walkers should continue ahead past the Roman Villa (right) ONLY if intending to visit Lullingstone Castle or church which lie at the end of a private metalled drive. Walkers visiting the Castle or church may usually continue beyond the Castle (left) and along a riverside track, although this is not a public footpath, to Kingfisher Bridge to rejoin the Walk which comes over the bridge from the left.

LULLINGSTONE CASTLE belongs to the Hart Dyke family. The Castle gatehouse is Tudor and was here when Henry VIII and Catherine of Aragon came to stay. St Botolph's, known as 'the church on the lawn', is a parish church. The nave is Norman and the screen is decorated with Queen Catherine's pomegranate symbol and peach stones in recognition of Sir John Peche, Henry VIII's jousting champion who lived at the Castle. The estate passed to Sir John's nephew Sir Percyval Hart and in 1738 the heiress Anne Hart married Sir Thomas Dyke. Anne Hart's father frequently entertained Queen Anne here and during this period the house was rebuilt. The treads on the Grand Staircase are shallow; this was to assist the Queen who had difficulty with stairs. She left two chests and a doll here and the ruins of her bath house can be seen behind the main house. In 1873 the rules of lawn tennis were devised on the lawn by Sir William Hart Dyke and his friends. The unique Lullingstone Silk Farm, now in Dorset, was begun here in 1932 by Zoë Lady Hart Dyke and it was following a visit by Queen Mary that it became customary for the farm to supply silk for royal wedding dresses. The Castle and grounds are open between April and September on Saturdays, Sundays and Bank Holidays from 2.00 to 6.00pm; admission £1.50, pensioners £1.00 and children 75p. The grounds only are open Wednesdays to Fridays during the summer; admission £1.00, pensioners and children 75p. The public may enter the gateway to visit the church on any day and on open days may picnic in the grounds.

Lullingstone's 'church on the lawn'

Those not intending to visit Lullingstone Castle should cross the River Darent by the Roman Villa and follow a partly metalled lane to a gateway on the main road. There is usually a tea stall in the lay-by opposite. Turn right uphill to pass the eastern entrance to Lullingstone Castle. After a short distance bear right into the straight Castle Road which leads to Kingfisher Bridge and a sharp bend.

Soon the road passes Castle Farm — site of Shoreham Castle. Keep ahead where the lane turns sharply to the right. The footpath runs on top of a bank with hop fields to the left and an orchard on the right. At the far end of the bank go ahead through a line of trees and across a field to go over a concrete path. Keep forward through a gap in the hedge and bear half left across a field which gently rises to the centre. In the far corner of the field go over a broken stile by a gap. There is a glimpse of the river (left). Keep by the wire fence (left) and at the end of the field go over a wooden stile to follow a narrow path by the river (left).

On reaching the end of a metalled lane turn left towards the entrance to a converted mill and at once go right along a short path which crosses the river. Turn right along the metalled

Shoreham Bridge

riverside path to follow the water (right). The path leads past Water House into the centre of Shoreham.

The Walk continues to the left (not over the bridge) up the road to pass Ivy Cottage (left). Keep forward through the lychgate and up the brick church path (laid in 1881). Beyond the church (left) go through the kissing gate and turn right to reach the road opposite Shoreham Place. Turn left up the road.

To reach Shoreham Station go ahead.

To continue the Walk turn right, before the railway bridge, on to a footpath which runs between wooden barriers and along a thin belt of trees. Keep ahead on this mainly fenced path which runs across a golf course and reaches a wooden kissing gate at a cricket field. The path runs ahead, within the game's boundary, to pass through a broken gateway to the left of the cricket pavilion.

The fenced path has a grass surface as far as a junction of paths where the way, which still runs ahead, becomes chalky. Beyond the end of the golf course and a wood (right) there is a clear view over the valley to Sepham Farm's three oast houses which were known to Palmer.

SHOREHAM means 'home in the cleft'. The church tower was built in 1775 but the church itself is a much enlarged and changed Norman building. The screen, as at Lullingstone, displays Catherine of Aragon's pomegranate emblem. The pulpit stood in the choir of Westminster Abbey for over 20 years in the nineteenth century and the much older organ case also comes from the Abbey. In the south wall there is a window by Burne-Jones in memory of Sir Joseph Prestwich, the geologist, who lived at Darenthulme in Schacklands Road. Harold Copping, the Bible illustrator, who lived at The Studio in Crown Road, and Lord Dunsany, the poet who lived at Dunstall Priory in the woods to the east, are both buried to the north-west of the church. Former incumbents here include two Cardinals and Nicholas Heath, Archbishop of York and Lord Chancellor under Mary I. Vincent Perronet, vicar from 1728 to 1785, was a friend of John Wesley who often preached in the churchyard. Vincent's son, Edward, wrote the hymn 'All hail the power of Jesus' name!' Artist Samuel Palmer was steeped in the Bible when he came in 1824 to stay at Ivy Cottage in the main street between the church and the river. He was escaping from London, which he called 'that great dust hole', and the following year bought Water House. Palmer and his friends roamed the valley footpaths at night and that year he produced 'Early Morning' showing a rabbit on a footpath. Another picture he described with words from Psalm 65: 'The folds shall be full of sheep: the valleys also shall stand so thick with corn, that they shall laugh and sing.' When he left the village in 1832 Palmer had completed his best work — much of which can be seen at Oxford's Ashmolean Museum although the Yale Centre for British Art has the better picture of Ivy Cottage. The village teashop has now closed, but on Saturdays and Sundays from Easter to September The Shoreham Society serves a buffet tea between 3.00 and 5.00pm at Bridge House where Palmer postcards may also be purchased. Next door there is The King's Arms which has a well-preserved ostler's box.

Hops

Soon, there is a view of Otford Church ahead. The path begins to run downhill and then widens when joined by another from the right. Beyond two converted oast houses (left) the track becomes metalled and runs into Otford. The village centre and The Willow Tea Room are to the left, on the Pilgrims' Way.

Otford Station is in Station Road (marked Pilgrims' Way) beyond the pond (right).

Otford Palace

OTFORD. When King Canute and Edmund Ironside clashed here in 1016 the river is said to have been red with blood. The ruined Otford Palace was built by Archbishop Warham who crowned Henry VIII and Catherine of Aragon. The King stayed here on his way to the Field of the Cloth of Gold and also when his first divorce was being considered. In the church Catherine's pomegranate is to be found in the Easter sepulchre to the left of the high altar. In the vestry there is a pre-Reformation oven for baking communion wafers. The church is still candlelit although electricity has been installed. The church hall (opposite The Bull) was designed in 1909 by Edwin Lutyens when his brother was the vicar. The Willow Tea Room, opposite the pond, is open daily including weekends until 5.00pm.

Walk 7
DOWNE AND CHEVENING

Downe — Knockholt — Chevening —
Knockholt — Cudham — Downe

5- or 10-mile circular walk   OS sheets 187 & 188

Paths in this part of Kent are usually free of obstacles and signposted, thanks to the well-known vigilance of local walking groups. The Walk starts and finishes outside a village church where the last bus stop on a Red Bus route stands by its west wall. This figure-of-8 Walk offers a shorter alternative to the full outing round the highest village in Kent and the Chevening estate below. Although there are two pubs in Knockholt offering refreshment, the views from the nearby Chevening paths are best enjoyed over a picnic. On two occasions the Walk briefly joins the 150-mile North Downs Way which opened in 1978 but is based on the ancient Winchester—Canterbury Pilgrims' Way.

Red Bus 146 runs from Bromley North British Rail Station and Bromley South British Rail Station to Downe about once an hour on Mondays to Saturdays. There is no bus service to Downe on Sundays or Bank Holidays. Bromley South can be reached in less than 20 minutes from Victoria whilst Bromley North is served by a shuttle train from Grove Park on the Charing Cross Line. There is parking space behind Downe Church in High Elms road. London Country Bus 471 (daily except Sundays) runs in a circle from Orpington and calls at Cudham and Knockholt.

Walk up Cudham Road by the church (left) and The George & Dragon. After 300 yards, just beyond the gateway (right) to Downe Court, there is a footpath running parallel to the road. Follow this path which runs just above the road for ½ mile. Where the path rejoins the road turn right along the road for a

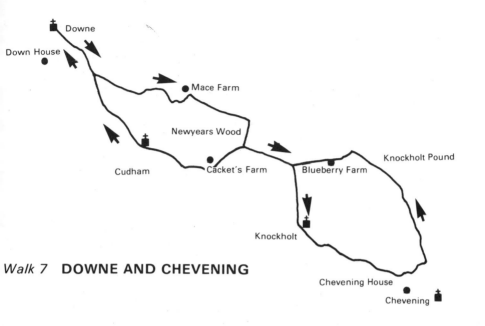

Walk 7 DOWNE AND CHEVENING

few yards and then turn left on to a wide path to pass Hangrove Cottage (left).

Follow the fenced way which bears left down the wooded hill. Where the wire fence on the right gives way to a wooden fence turn right to follow a steeper path which becomes stepped. The enclosed narrow path continues across a valley and climbs the opposite hill to enter another wood. At a wooden stile turn left with the new wire fence. After a bend the path widens and when level becomes metalled by The Shaws Girl Guide Camp Site. Continue along the lane to meet Cudham Lane.

Turn left (with care) to pass the high wall of Hostye Lodge (right). At the end of the Lodge's garden turn right to leave the lane and cross a wooden stile into a field. Follow the hedge (right) which ends at another corner. Cross the stile and go ahead up the field towards a gate by a telegraph pole. (Mace Farm can be seen to the left.) Go through the gate and turn left along the metalled Mace Lane.

Walk past Mace Farm House (left) and on approaching the white farm cottages turn right to go over a wooden stile between two gates. Follow the hedge and fence (right) along

63

the side of the field to a wooden stile by a wooden gate. There is a view over a ridge into a valley. Keep forward downhill to the wooden stile on the edge of Kangles Wood. The footpath then runs to the right in a half circle up the bank ahead. At the top of the slope go half left through the trees to a stile on the far side of the wood.

After crossing the stile go half right up the field to just miss the thin line of trees at the field corner (left). Pass an almost hidden pond (right) by Newyears Wood and follow the trees (right) round a corner to a wooden stile. The Newyears Wood path bends and soon runs in a straight line to a stile by New Years Cottage.

DOWNE. The 'e' was added to avoid confusion with County Down in Northern Ireland but Down House, where Charles Darwin lived and died, retains the old spelling. Here the naturalist worked on *The Origin of Species* and in 1876 received a visit from Gladstone. The house is open daily except for Mondays and Fridays and the whole of February, from 1.00 to 6.00pm; admission 75p, children 20p. The church, probably built in the thirteenth century and now used by both Anglicans and Roman Catholics, has a fifteenth-century tower. Elizabeth I attended a baptism here in the second year of her reign. In the chancel floor there is a memorial to Edward Manning who was page to Prince Charles, the future Charles I. On the south chancel wall there is a plaque to John Lubbock (Lord Avebury) who invented Bank Holidays and who ceased to attend this church when his friend Darwin was attacked from the pulpit. Robin Knox-Johnston's 1968–9 round-the-world voyage is commemorated by a window to the right of the high altar. The east window is by Evie Hone (*see page 21*). This remote village is, surprisingly, within the GLC area and part of the London borough of Bromley. Both The Queen's Head and The George & Dragon are well known for food and on Sundays and Bank Holidays (between April and September) teas are served in the village hall (opposite the bus stop) between 3.00 and 5.00pm.

Down House

Downe

Those not attempting the full walk should turn right here (see page 70).

The main Walk continues past the cottage, which lies on a double bend in New Years Lane. Go over the stile ahead and at once bear left into the thin trees of Birches Croft. The path winds and becomes very narrow before reaching a wooden stile where there is a view across a shallow valley. Go half left across the field and on reaching the far side follow the now steeper path down the short side (left) of the field to a corner. Here, turn left into the trees and go down a short and very steep slope to a stile.

Go into the field and follow the hedge (right) up the hill. Before reaching the top turn right over a stile. Try to keep near the wire fence (right) on walking through the copse to enter a field. Turn half left to walk up the sloping field. Keep ahead towards the trees to find a stile in a corner by some holly bushes.

Keep ahead, following field boundaries (left), over two further stiles to pass a wall (left). At the end of the wall go over a stile by a wooden gate and head across a field towards Knockholt Church. Cross a stile to enter the churchyard.

On the far side of the churchyard turn right along Knockholt

KNOCKHOLT, once Ocolte, means 'corner of an oak wood' and is the highest village in Kent. The church, where both Anglican and Roman Catholic services are held, dates from 1281 but probably stands on the site of a Norman chapel. On the south side there is a window erected in memory of Susanna Thrale who lived at Ash Grove (*see page 69*) at Knockholt Pound where she brought the summerhouse (*see page 25*) used by Dr Johnson at the Thrales' Streatham garden. Ash Grove was later the home of William Wells, founder of the Royal Society of Painters in Watercolours and a friend of Turner who visited about 1800 and recorded local scenes here including the inside of Wells' kitchen. Knockholt Station (2 miles to the east) is thought to have inspired Edith Nesbit to write *The Railway Children.*

Main Road to reach The Crown (left). Go over the stile at the side of the pub and follow the enclosed path which continues over open ground. Beyond a wooden stile walk ahead across a large field keeping to the left of the Knockholt Clumps. On reaching the hedge on the far side turn left to briefly join the North Downs Way and follow the hedge (right) towards a stile by Sundridge Lane.

Go over the stile (where there is a steep drop) into the lane. Turn right and follow the lane past two Chevening Estate cottages. At the second cottage turn left to enter a drive and go over a hidden stile by a wooden gate.

Keep forward up a wide fenced grass path which soon enters Park Wood. After ¼ mile the way bears half right and begins to run downhill to a seat at a viewpoint. The path continues downhill to a small wooden gate and enters a field. Follow a fence (left) on the edge of the wood. Beyond a stile by a gate ahead there is the first clear view of Chevening House.

Chevening

Keep along the side of the field to go through an iron kissing gate and join a farm track at a bend. Keep forward with the wood (left). Before the path bears left there is a view of the Pilgrims' Way passing the house.

On approaching an iron gate turn right to follow a wire fence (left). When the way is level with the front of the mansion (right) look left up into the trees to see the 'keyhole' view through the wood. Go over a stile to cross a carriage drive and continue alongside the fence (left). Go over a stile at the end of the fence and follow the trees (right) round a bend. Go over two stiles at another estate road. Follow the wire fence (right) where there is a view beyond of Chevening Church's fifteenth-century tower. Cross a wooden stile to turn left on to an enclosed path known locally as Break Neck. Until 1792 the

---

CHEVENING. The mansion was designed by Inigo Jones in 1630 and the two wings were added in 1740 by the first Earl Stanhope, the Foreign Secretary, who had bought the house in 1717. Later the third Earl closed the Pilgrims' Way, which runs across the front of the building, and diverted the nearby main road (*see page 69*). Visitors have included William Pitt the Elder, the Duke of Wellington, Lord Rosebery who described Chevening as 'paradise' and Kipling who thought it 'enchanted'. George VI and Neville Chamberlain were both guests of the last Earl Stanhope who died in 1967 leaving the 3,000-acre estate for use as an official residence. The Chevening Estate Act lays down that if the Royal Family and the Cabinet have no use for the house then it passes to the Canadian High Commissioner or the US Ambassador. It was to prevent this happening that Lord Hailsham took up temporary residence in the servants' quarters in 1973. The following year Prince Charles announced his intention to live here and so fulfil Lord Stanhope's greatest wish. However, in spite of his early intentions to work on the garden and eventually use the house as a family home, Prince Charles gave up the idea shortly before his engagement to Lady Diana Spencer. For the present, Chevening has become the Foreign Secretary's official country house.

The old main road at Chevening

main London road ran parallel to the left. Beyond a seat there is a kissing gate.

The path, no longer enclosed, crosses a stile and follows the fence (left) as the way begins to climb. To the south (behind) there is another view of the church. The path crosses a wooden stile and becomes enclosed again as the way climbs through the wood. After a steep climb the way runs into the open and crosses a wooden stile where the Walk again joins the North Downs Way. Turn on to the end of Chevening Lane (the old main road) to pass a house (left) and the North Downs Way stile. Continue along the metalled lane to pass Ash Grove (right) just before reaching Knockholt Pound. To the left there is The Three Horseshoes and the village shop.

Keep forward past the bus stop (right) to cross Knockholt Main Road and go up the road ahead known as both Pound Lane and Bond Street. Follow the lane for just over ¼ mile to the crossroads at Singles Cross.

Go left and after 150 yards climb over a wooden stile (right) by a gate. Walk half left across the field to a stile behind a rusty corrugated iron shed on the edge of Blueberry Farm. At once turn right to walk towards a wooden stile by a gate.

Beyond the stile bear half left to pass between the bottom of the bank in the field (right) and the trees (left). Bear left with the trees and in the corner enter a (usually) muddy enclosure where there is a wooden stile (left).

Cross the stile and at once turn right with the fence. After a short distance go over another stile (right). Climb half left up the steep field to find a further wooden stile by a pond at the top. Cross the stile and continue half left across the sloping field to a stile in the hedge.

Here you join the outward route so do not cross the stile but follow the hedge (left) downhill and up to the stile in the trees ahead. Climb up the steep slope beyond and turn right up the side of the field to the corner. Bear half left across the centre of the field. Cross the wooden stile and follow the winding path through Birches Croft to emerge at the stile by New Years Cottage. Pass the cottage and go left through a wooden gate.

Those on the short Walk will have come over the stile on the north side of the cottage to go through the gate.

Once inside the gate do not take the clear track to the right but keep forward on the bridleway which runs south-west through Newyears Wood and forms the boundary between Kent (left) and the GLC area. After ¼ mile the path runs downhill to pass between the edge of the wood and a field. On high ground to the right is Cacket's Farm. On coming level with the end of the farm buildings turn right to go over a stile and follow a wire fence (right). Go over another stile to join Cacket's Lane at a bend.

Keep forward to pass Cacket's Farm (right) and walk along the hedged lane for 375 yards to cross a stile on the right just before Cottage Farm (left). Go half left over the field towards Cudham Church. Cross a stile and continue in the same direction to find an iron kissing gate below a house. Beyond the

---

CUDHAM. Although the church was greatly restored in 1892 it dates from about 953 and the original building remains as the south chapel. In the churchyard are two huge yews which are probably even older than the church. Newly married couples leave the church to what may be the lightest peal of bells in the old Kent county.

70

Cudham Church

gate follow an enclosed footpath by a wall (right) to emerge on a playing field. Go half right across the grass to reach the churchyard and walk along a metalled path past Cudham Church (right).

Walk down Church Approach to the road junction. There are bus stops to the right. Cross the road with care to go down Church Hill. Do not take the sharp turning to Biggin Hill but keep ahead round the steep but more gentle bend. The road runs downhill. At the end of a gap in the trees on the left go over an easily missed stile to cut a corner off the road walk. Walk half right across the field towards the corner below the wooded hill. Go through a gap in the trees (where there may be a strand of wire to negotiate) to rejoin the road at a bend. Turn left to walk up Hangrove Hill beneath the trees of Hang Grove. At the top of the hill the road runs by Hangrove Cottage (right) which was passed on the outward route.

After a few yards take the footpath (left) which runs parallel to the road. Where the path ends follow the road into Downe.

Walk 8
EPSOM DOWNS

Tattenham Corner — Walton on the Hill —
Headley — Tattenham Corner

6½-mile circular walk   OS sheet 187

The Derby was first run on Epsom Downs in 1780 after Lord
Derby and Sir Thomas Bunbury had tossed a coin to decide
which of them should give their name to the race. Derby Day is
always on the first Wednesday in June and the traditional
gipsy village gathers on preceding days. Admission to the
Downs remains free and over ¼ million people are drawn here
by the 2½-minute race and the fun fair, fortune-tellers and
jellied-eel stalls. This is still the Londoners' day out and open-
top buses line the course near the finishing post opposite the
grandstand. At one time Parliament used to adjourn for the

Epsom race course

72

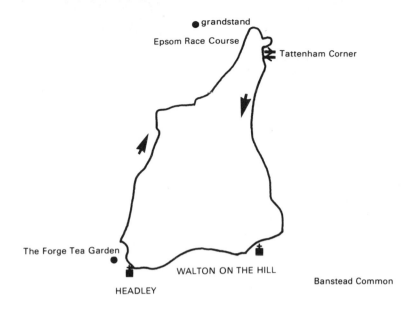

grandstand

Epsom Race Course

Tattenham Corner

The Forge Tea Garden

WALTON ON THE HILL

Banstead Common

HEADLEY

Walk 8 EPSOM DOWNS

entire week while the London clubs and the Army and Navy
Stores had their own marquees. Charles Dickens, describing
the lunchtime scene, wrote 'And now Heavens! All the
hampers fly wide open and green Downs burst into a blossom
of Lobster Salad!' For most of the year the Downs are empty
and a walk both in and out of Derby Week is recommended.

TATTENHAM CORNER. The station was opened on
Derby Day 1901. The now rather diminished mound outside the station, which affords a fine view of the race
course below, was used by the railway directors to watch
the Derby. It was here during the 1913 Derby that suffra-
gette Emily Davidson dashed in front of the King's horse
Anmer. Although Miss Davidson died from her injuries
her act was probably not intended as suicide since a day-
return ticket was found in her pocket. The Queen and other
members of the Royal Family arrive here in the Royal
Train each Derby Day.

Trains run from Charing Cross via East Croydon to British Rail's Tattenham Corner Station on Epsom Downs.

On leaving Tattenham Corner Station turn left and left again to pass round the back of the grass mound. Beyond the double iron gates cross Epsom Lane and turn left to follow the road (left). Half right there is a view of Headley's church spire (*see page 77*) in the trees. Go under a wooden barrier and continue ahead as the way (now a rough path) becomes separated from the road by a hedge. The path runs gently downhill and bears half right.

Where the way widens keep by the hedge (left). Soon after Headley's spire (ahead) disappears from view bear left with the

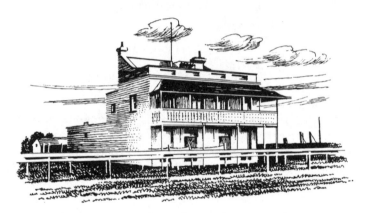

Prince's stand

bridleway as it enters the trees. Ignore all turnings and keep ahead. After passing a line of white posts the path narrows and climbs uphill. For ½ mile the path runs between gardens (left) and fields (right) to emerge by stables at Motts Hill Lane.

Turn right along the unmetalled road which begins to climb at the bend. After a short distance leave the lane, which bends right, and keep ahead up an enclosed path at the side of the gateway to Derry. The enclosed way climbs steeply to a junction of paths by Mottshill Cottage (left). Keep ahead beyond a white barrier to enter Banstead Common. The foot-

Walton on the Hill pond

WALTON ON THE HILL. The church, although heavily restored, dates from 1268, the tower being rebuilt in the nineteenth century. The Norman font is probably the oldest in the country and was brought here from another church. The painting above the Lady Chapel altar is a copy of 'The Immaculate Conception of the Escorial' by Murillo in Madrid. The Bible is attached to the lectern by a medieval chain from Salisbury Cathedral. The unusual art nouveau lamps feature St Peter's keys. Until as recently as 1927 the village was in the Diocese of Winchester and in 1896 part of the churchyard was consecrated by the Bishop of Southampton. Anthony Hope, author of *The Prisoner of Zenda*, lived and died at Heath Farm (beyond The Blue Ball in Deans Lane) but is buried at Leatherhead (*see page 80*). There is no café in the village but the newsagent (opposite The Fox and Hounds) and The Little Shoppe (opposite The Chequers) sell filled bread rolls.

path ahead leads to The Bell and a row of cottages at Withybed Corner. Continue forward on a rough lane to meet a main road. Turn right with Mere Pond (right) to walk through Walton on the Hill.

Bear left with the main street and before reaching The Chequers (left) turn right into Queen's Close. At Walton Manor Farm (left) the metalled surface gives way to a path which, after 300 yards, narrows and bends as the way runs downhill on the edge of a wood. There is a brief glimpse of Headley's church spire (half left). At the bottom of the hill the path runs out into the open to meet a cross path.

Turn left and take the narrow stony way to follow the side of Great Hurst Wood (right) which is on the route of the proposed M25 road. When the field (left) gives way to a fir wood, the path becomes enclosed by trees. After 100 yards (and whilst still in the wood) bear half right on to a narrower way which climbs through the trees to reach a wooden stile. Ahead there is a clear view of Headley Church. Cross the stile and walk over the field towards the church to find another wooden stile near the churchyard entrance.

To continue the Walk, follow the enclosed footpath which runs along the east side of the churchyard. (Those visiting the church can join this path from the north-east corner of the churchyard.) From the footpath there are glimpses of the Grandstand on Epsom Downs (half right). Where the path divides turn right. If it is a Sunday, you can go ahead and then turn right to visit The Forge Tea Garden (*see page 77*). The main path meets Hurst Lane beyond iron barriers.

Turn right along Hurst Lane and continue for nearly ¼ mile to a crescent of houses (right). Where the houses end and the road bends, bear half left to a stables' entrance. Take the enclosed footpath which runs north from a tree by the gateway. (This path also may eventually be bisected by the M25.) At the end of the long and almost straight path turn right to the road. Go left up the road for a few yards and at North Lodge (left) turn right on to a wide path known as Sheep Walk.

The wide wooded path narrows slightly as the way begins to run downhill. At the bottom of the hill do not go ahead at the fork but bear left to join another track (from the right). At once

Headley Church gate

HEADLEY means 'clearing in the heather' and was called Hallega in the Domesday Book. Later spellings included Hedleigh and Hedley before the present form was adopted in 1899. The old church, dating from the fourteenth century, was replaced by the present building in the 1850s. The tower is built of materials from the previous church which stood to the south as indicated by the yew trees. Charles II's Royal Arms are inside on the west wall and the nave panelling, given by Lord Cunliffe of Headley who lived at Headley Court, was brought from Newgate Prison when the Old Bailey was erected on the site. William Hardcastle, the broadcaster and journalist, is buried in the south-west corner of the churchyard from where there is a view of his home, the whitewashed Webb's Farm, for which he had to pay a yearly rent (equal to a sack of wheat) for the benefit of the parish poor. The Forge Tea Garden on the corner of Church and Hurst Lanes is open on Sundays. Near the church there is the eighteenth-century Cock Inn.

Epsom Downs

bear half right on to a more minor path which climbs gently through a wood. On emerging in the open, at a junction of several paths, keep ahead up a track. To the right there is the grass of Walton Downs and soon there is a hedge on the left. At the top of the hill, the path turns into a wood to run just inside the trees.

After 300 yards the woodland path turns left. Just before passing a lonely cottage (left) turn right to follow a wide path which, after a bend, runs out into the open. At the far end the track becomes metalled and crosses Epsom race course. (The metalled path is covered with mats and cut grass on race days.) Do not bear right with the road but keep ahead on a rough track to cross Epsom Downs. Tattenham Corner can be seen to the right. On crossing the course again keep ahead to a road junction near the Downs keepers' hut (left) and a tea stall (across the road ahead and open daily). Turn right to reach Tattenham Corner Station.

Walk 9
BOX HILL

Leatherhead — Mickleham — Box Hill —
Mickleham — Leatherhead

8½-mile circular walk   OS sheet 187

This circular Walk forms the shape of a 6 with the climax on
Box Hill, which is so carefully preserved by the National Trust
that the past literary figures who knew the area would not feel
lost today. The first stage of the route follows the River Mole
upstream. The Mole rises by Gatwick Airport and flows into
the Thames at Hampton Court by way of Stoke d'Abernon,
Painshill Park and Esher. Edmund Spenser, Michael Drayton,
John Milton and Alexander Pope all referred to the Mole in
their writings. During droughts it is possible to walk along the
river bed whilst water flows below in the chalk's 'swallow
holes'. Pope witnessed this and wrote of 'the sullen Mole, that
hides his driving flood' and Spenser suggested that the river
was 'like the mousing mole' who made 'His way still underground till Thames he overtake'. The paths here are mostly in
good condition but there are very steep climbs before the
panoramic views can be enjoyed.

Red buses no longer serve Leatherhead, which is just outside
the GLC area, but trains from Waterloo and Victoria call at
Leatherhead British Rail Station. Green Line Bus 714 from
Victoria to Dorking stops at Leatherhead, Mickleham and Box
Hill. There is also a railway station (Box Hill and West
Humble) near Burford Bridge.

The Walk begins at the entrance to the Leisure Centre in
Guildford Road. Those arriving at Leatherhead Station should
walk down Station Approach and cross the main road at the
pelican crossing to follow a footpath on the east side of the
railway line. Keep ahead to follow Waterway Road (there is a

79

view of the old bridge to the left) to a junction with Guildford Road (where there is a crossing under the railway bridge). Bus travellers should alight in the town centre and walk down Bridge Street to cross the old bridge.

Walk up the road leading to the Leatherhead Leisure Centre. Where the road bears right to the Centre, keep forward to pass the Centre (right). There is a view of Leatherhead church tower (left). Go through a wooden kissing gate to cross an unmetalled lane and climb over a long stile between brick walls.

The wall on the right falls away to reveal open country. Beyond a wooden stile the path leaves the field boundary (left) and curves gently to the right to join the bank of the River Mole. After crossing an iron stile the way runs under the new Young Street Bridge.

Cross a stile (to enter Norbury Park) and keep along the edge of the river on a short enclosed path to another riverside stile. Whilst the river swings to the left, the footpath runs ahead with a clear view of the parallel railway line (right). As the river

---

LEATHERHEAD. The Guildford road crosses the River Mole on a fourteen-arch brick bridge built in 1782 and widened during George IV's reign. Nearby there is a twentieth-century bridge and two fine sets of railway arches. By the approach to the old bridge there is The Running Horse which is featured in Thomas Skelton's poem 'The Tunnyng of Elynour Rumming', written about 1517. On a hill above the river is the partly Saxon church of St Mary and St Nicholas which owes its rare dedication to the Priory of that name at Leeds in Kent which received from Edward III the right to nominate the incumbent here. The fifteenth-century tower had a spire until 1703. Anthony Hope (*see page 75*) is buried in the north-east corner of the churchyard. The Mole Valley District Council offices on Bull Hill stand on the site of Kingston House where in 1791 John Wesley preached the last of his many sermons. When Richard Brinsley Sheridan, the dramatist, rented Randalls Farm in 1808 he joined a fishing party 'on our River Mole'.

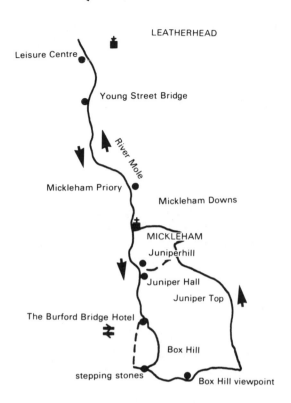

Walk 9 **BOX HILL**

swings back the footpath begins to rise and the bank becomes wooded. The way then runs downhill through a sloping wood to cross a stile by a wooden gate.

Keep ahead on the track which turns left by a cottage to pass

YOUNG STREET BRIDGE, opened in 1978, replaces a Bailey Bridge which was erected a few yards to the north in 1941 by the Royal Canadian Engineers. The original bridge was opened by Mackenzie King, the Canadian Prime Minister who defeated Richard Bennett (*see page 83*) in 1935. This new bridge was opened by the Canadian High Commissioner.

81

near the river again. The track becomes metalled before passing through a wooden gate. A farm road joins from the left before the way passes several buildings including Mickleham Priory (left) which hides the river. Continue along the fenced and metalled road which bears right and left to cross the Mole and meet the Mickleham by-pass. Cross the dual carriageway with care and walk up Mickleham's main street.

Continue south between the church and the village shop by

MICKLEHAM. There are traces of Saxon work in the Norman church which has been heavily restored. The slightly off-set east end is a 'weeping chancel' representing Christ's head on the cross. The font is Norman and the oak panelling in the Norbury Chapel came from St Paul's School after being saved from the Great Fire of London. Among the restored funeral hatchments recently placed in the church are the arms of Sir Lucas Pepys (last on north side of nave; *see page 16*). The church was the scene of Fanny Burney's and General D'Arblay's wedding on a July Sunday morning in 1793; here also George Meredith, the novelist and poet, married his second wife in 1864. Lord Bennett (*see page 83*) often read the lesson at services (although he was a Methodist) and is now buried outside the main door. The pub sign opposite shows the 1828 Derby winner; the horse was stabled here and won the race only after a re-run between two joint winners. John Stuart Mill, the economist and philosopher, had a summer home behind the old post office (a post box remains) at the side of the pub from 1830 to 1857. The village was, then an hour's ride by horse-drawn coach from the Elephant & Castle — the modern Green Line Bus takes longer than this to come from Victoria. Mill sometimes came with his father or a friend such as the historian Thomas Carlyle. Whilst here he would often wander along the lanes scattering seeds he had collected in France. Talbot Village in Dorset was founded by the Talbot sisters who came from here and cottages in the model village resemble some of the Mickleham houses.

Mickleham Church

walking along the pavement on the right of the road. After a long wall (right) there is a short stretch of iron railing before the path becomes separated from the road by a hedge. The footpath runs just below the road (left) to pass Juniperhill and Juniper Hall (left) at a junction.

JUNIPERHILL dates from 1780 and was the last home of Richard Bennett, Prime Minister of Canada from 1930 to 1935. He bought the house from Lord Beaverbrook (he once worked in the same Canadian law practice) who lived at nearby Cherkley Court. Bennett's butler had worked as a footman at 10 Downing Street during Asquith's premiership. On Sunday evenings villagers were invited in to watch the latest films which had been sent down the hill from Beaverbrook's house. When Bennett was made a peer in 1941 he took the title Viscount Bennett of Mickleham, Surrey, and of Calgary and Hopewell, Canada. He died here in 1947.

JUNIPER HALL is now owned by the National Trust and occupied by the Field Studies Council. Most of the present building dates from about 1770 although the exterior is nineteenth-century. A group of French émigrés, including the Count de Narbonne, Talleyrand, Madame de Staël and General D'Arblay who had been Adjutant General to Lafayette, rented the house after the French Revolution. D'Arblay got to know Fanny Burney (who had just resigned with a pension of £100 a year as Queen Charlotte's Second Keeper of the Robes) when they tried to teach each other their own languages in the drawing room.

BURFORD BRIDGE. The hotel began as The Fox & Hounds but was already known as The Burford Bridge Hotel by 1856. Lord Nelson was one of the first guests in 1801 and described the location as 'a very pretty place'. Keats (*see page 26*) came in 1817 when he found his landlord's children at Hampstead too noisy. On his first night he took a moonlit walk up Box Hill and then spent just over two weeks finishing 'Endymion' in a back room overlooking the stableyard. Byron, Hazlitt, Sheridan and Wordsworth all knew this resting place on the old London–Dorking road. Robert Louis Stevenson, who mentions it in 'A Gossip on Romance', stayed twice and wrote part of the *New Arabian Nights* here. His friend George Meredith, who lived at nearby Flint Cottage, preferred to entertain his guests in the inn's garden. Hilaire Belloc wrote in *The Absence of the Past*: 'As you take the road to Paradise, about halfway there you come to an inn which even as inns go is admirable. You go into the garden of it and see the great wall of Box Hill shrouding you all around.' Royal visitors included Queen Victoria who stayed for several days as a young princess, Queen Amélia of Portugal who called for tea, and Queen Alexandra who declared that she had 'never seen a prettier place in my life'. Opposite the hotel, which has always been popular with honeymoon couples, are picnic tables and, in the car park, an excellent tea stall open from early morning until midnight.

Continue along the footpath to pass the entrance to the eighteenth-century Fredley Manor (often visited by John Stuart Mill) and then climb steeply above the road. After a short distance the path runs down some steps to a bus stop. Go ahead down the road. On reaching a T-junction you can continue on the pavement or cross the road to follow a parallel path along the top of the bank (left). The path runs down to the road again opposite the Burford Bridge picnic site.

From Burford Bridge there is a choice of route. Those who wish to avoid a narrow and sometimes slippery path high above the river, should go beyond the hotel and walk south along the dual carriageway. (To reach Box Hill Station go through the subway and turn left and then right up a lane.) After less than ½ mile turn left on to a track (signposted North Downs Way) which crosses the Mole by stepping stones (see below). A bridge downstream should be used if the water is high.

The main Walk from Burford Bridge is up the steep path from the bus stop at the side of the hotel. Do not turn right with the hotel's wire fence but a few yards on bear right where the way divides. After a few more yards turn right on to a long straight path. (At this junction there is a half-hidden stone in the ground indicating the direct way to the top of the hill.)

The straight path runs south along a narrow ledge on the side of the wooded cliff. There is a glimpse of the hotel below and then an almost sheer drop down to the river. Occasional tree felling sometimes causes odd diversions along the way. After ½ mile the path quickly drops down to the river to pass a footbridge. Keep by the river to reach the stepping stones.

Turn left and away from the river to follow the North Downs

STEPPING STONES. This crossing is traditionally considered to be part of the ancient Pilgrims' Way (*see page 62*) and is now on the modern North Downs Way. The present set of stones was presented in 1946 by Chuter Ede who was Home Secretary and lived at Epsom, and the reconstructed footway was inaugurated by the Prime Minister, Clement Attlee.

Stepping stones

Way. After the path begins to rise keep right (as indicated by the waymark) up a very steep woodland path. There is a view (right) down through the trees to the river before the way-marked route turns left to go steeply up the hill. The wide path bears right. Take the left fork with the last waymark. Wooden borders define the path through the trees. There are two flights of steps on this long wooded path before the way reaches a cross path. At once turn right to step into the open near the top of Box Hill. On a clear day Dorking can be seen below.

Follow the well-defined path which bears left with the trees

BOX HILL. From here there is a view over Dorking, Brockham and Betchworth below. Chanctonbury Ring is on the South Downs ahead. Jane Austen came here and made it the setting for one of the unsuccessful picnics in *Emma*. There is a National Trust shop and information centre discreetly placed among the trees. Next door is a refreshment hut (open daily in the summer and from 10.00am to 5.00pm on winter weekends) and, surprisingly, a new restaurant. Early last century water had to be carried up from the river in order to serve teas to visitors.

North Downs Way path

and bushes (left) to reach the stone viewpoint at the summit.
From the viewpoint turn to walk over to the road behind.
(Turn left for the shop and refreshments.) The Walk continues
to the right (in an easterly direction) along the road. There is a
footpath on the right and more views through the trees (right).

On approaching Upper Farm on the edge of Box Hill village
(there is a tea garden to the right) turn left just before the barn
to follow a bridleway into the trees. Take the right fork where
the way divides after 300 yards but otherwise ignore all
turnings and just follow the path through the wood for ½ mile.
The wide path narrows before emerging into the open on
Juniper Top. Ahead are the wooded Mickleham Downs.

Walk down the hill with the view unfolding. Soon Juniper
Hall can be seen ahead on the left in the valley. Towards the
bottom of the hill the wide grass area narrows and a path runs
ahead through trees to join a bridleway. Turn right to reach a
road.

*Those who do not wish to face the exceptionally steep path
ahead should turn left along the road to reach Juniper Hall and
then go right at the junction to reach Mickleham Church.*

The Walk continues between the wooden barriers on the far
side of the road and up the very steep path. At the top of the
hill the path turns right and soon runs into the open giving a

Box Hill viewpoint

Woodland near Leatherhead

view of Juniper Top (right). When the path re-enters the trees keep on the main path and after a few yards turn sharp left round an iron corner post. After a few yards turn right with the path but take only a few paces before turning left on to another woodland path.

Soon the way runs gently downhill to cross a main track by an iron gateway (left). There has been some felling here recently. Continue ahead on the narrow path which runs more steeply downhill. Soon there is a view across a field (left) and at the bottom of the hill the path becomes enclosed for 200 yards before crossing a stile and joining a metalled drive. Follow the driveway to reach Mickleham.

Turn right to retrace the outward route to Leatherhead. Cross the dual carriageway to enter Norbury Park by the bridge over the Mole. Follow the metalled road and beyond the houses (right) bear left at a fork. The way becomes rough and turns sharply right by a cottage to pass through a wood. Beyond the trees the way becomes a footpath which touches the river by the new bridge and continues into Leatherhead.

Walk 10
THE THAMES TOWPATH
Putney — Barnes — Kew — Richmond

8¾ miles   OS sheet 176

This is a towpath walk along the River Thames from Putney to Richmond by way of Barnes and Kew with fine views of Hammersmith Mall, Chiswick, Strand-on-the-Green, Syon and Isleworth. Putney is the start of the Thames towpath which runs from here to the tiny hamlet of Inglesham in Wiltshire. Continuous walking along the entire river is impossible due to the loss of ferries at crucial crossing points but these first few miles are problem free and the richest in heritage of all the towpath which passes through six counties. The way is rural from the moment one crosses the Putney boundary and this Walk can be extended by continuing on to do part or all of the next Walk (*page 102*).

British Rail's trains run from Waterloo to Putney Station in the High Street; from here, turn right for the river. Putney Bridge Underground Station is on the Fulham bank and walkers should cross Putney Bridge (not the railway bridge walkway) to reach Putney Church. There are buses and BR trains at Barnes and Kew (which is also on the London Transport District Line). Richmond is at the end of the LT District Line and fast BR trains run from the same station to Waterloo via Putney.

From the south end of Putney Bridge walk upstream along Lower Richmond Road and after a short distance turn on to the Embankment. Just before the pier a stone engraved with the letters UBR marks the starting point for the annual Oxford and Cambridge Boat Race. Across the river are the Bishop's Park trees which screen the partly fifteenth-century Fulham Palace, once the home of the Bishops of London.

90

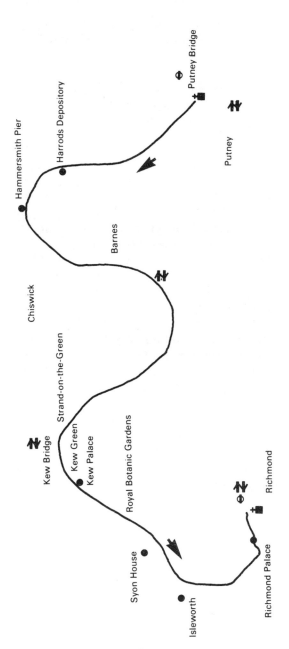

Walk 10 **THE THAMES TOWPATH**

The road ends at Beverley Brook which flows down into the Thames from Wimbledon Common and Richmond Park and here marks the boundary of Putney — once it was also the end of London and the beginning of Surrey. Beyond the footbridge the towpath is wide and rough. Soon there is the Boat Race mile post (left) and the way gradually narrows before reaching Harrods' Wharf by the famous Depository.

PUTNEY was once part of Wimbledon's parish although there has been a church here since at least the thirteenth century. St Mary's Church, by the Thames, has a fifteenth-century tower and contemporary arcading although, since a serious fire in 1973, much of the interior has been rebuilt and the high altar moved to the north side. The Bishop West Chapel (moved from the south side in the 1830s) was built by a local baker's son who became Bishop of Ely under Henry VIII and who, as Catherine of Aragon's chaplain, stood by the Queen during the divorce proceedings. In 1647, when Charles I was being held prisoner at Hampton Court, the New Model Army camped at Putney and Cromwell chaired the Putney Debates in the church. A new plaque (south side) recalls this first recorded public discussion of democratic principles which later influenced the drafting of the US Constitution. To the left of the organ there is a plaque to Edward Martyn who had Colonel Fleetwood (*see page 136*) billeted on him during the army's visit. At the beginning of the present century the Royal Standard was flown from the tower every Sunday in accordance with a privilege said to have been granted by Elizabeth I who visited Putney a dozen times and was grateful for shelter in the church during a thunderstorm. Samuel Pepys came to the church three times and left his hat under a pew. In 1737 Edward Gibbon, the historian, was baptised here. Charles Dickens also came and he used the church as the setting for David Copperfield's wedding. The original Putney Bridge, erected in 1729, was at that time the only Thames crossing between Kingston and London Bridge.

After a further 400 yards the towpath passes under Hammersmith Bridge (built in the 1880s). Soon there is a view across the water to Hammersmith Pier.

In another ¼ mile the towpath becomes level with Chiswick (right, across the water).

HARRODS' DEPOSITORY was erected in 1894 on the site of a candle factory. Once, families returning from the Empire would store their belongings here and live in a Harrods' flat at the back of the Brompton Road shop whilst looking for a permanent home. The Depository is linked by direct telephone line to the store and orders are often despatched direct to customers from here. A modern block was added in 1969. The river frontage is a famous Boat Race landmark and since the building has a similar silhouette to the Knightsbridge store it has been known to cause geographical confusion in the minds of television viewers when the commentator speaks of the crews 'passing Harrods'.

HAMMERSMITH PIER. To the left of the pier can be seen The Dove which started as a coffee house (visited by Charles II and Nell Gwynne) before becoming a pub; it was featured as The Pigeons in A. P. Herbert's novel *The Water Gipsies*. Farther to the left is Kelmscott House, home from 1878 to 1896 of designer and craftsman William Morris who had another Thames-side home in Oxfordshire.

CHISWICK. The eyot (or island), planted with willows which were once cut to make fish baskets, hides several period houses in Chiswick Mall. St Nicholas' Church has a fifteenth-century tower and in the riverside churchyard there is the tomb of William Hogarth, the painter and engraver.

Zoffany's tomb

BARNES. Barnes Common was mainly marshland until the late nineteenth century. The parish church, which is now closed following a very serious fire, is said to have been consecrated by Archbishop Langton shortly after he had secured King John's assent to Magna Carta. The church tower is late sixteenth-century and survives with its clock in working order. Strawberry House, next door, was built in the early eighteenth century as the rectory. Henry Fielding, the novelist, lived opposite the pond at Millbourne House from 1748 to 1752. The original house was built by William de Millebourne and behind the Georgian façade is a Jacobean staircase and an Elizabethan fireplace. Gustav Holst, the composer, lived at 10 Barnes Terrace from 1908 to 1913. Bennett's Delicatessen in Barnes High Street has a coffee bar and the Parish Bakery, opposite, sells take-away coffee.

The path, which enjoys various surfaces, runs on through trees, sometimes dividing then meeting up again. On approaching Barnes the way is metalled and then runs along the river side of Lonsdale Road to pass the end of Barnes High Street.

The Walk continues along the river with the eighteenth-century Barnes Terrace on the left. The path runs under Barnes Bridge (erected 1849) by the station (left). Beyond the bridge the way is grassed as far as Ye White Hart where the path becomes rough and often muddy, passing along the bottom of several gardens and across disused wharves. At The Ship, which overlooks the Boat Race finish, the way joins the metalled Thames Bank to pass several houses. Keep ahead with the river where the road bears slightly left and walk under Chiswick Bridge (erected only in 1933 and the first on this site).

For the next mile a mainly rough gravel path runs through trees. On approaching the five-arch Kew Railway Bridge (opened in 1896) there is a view (left) of the new Public Record Office and a glimpse of Strand-on-the-Green across the water.

Soon after passing a row of cottages (from where there is a clearer view over to Zoffany House) the towpath becomes metalled to pass Kew Pier and run under Kew Bridge (opened in 1903 as the Edward VII Bridge to replace an eighteenth-century bridge). A path (left) at the side of the new Kew Park Estate leads to Kew Green.

The Walk continues along the towpath which reverts to a gravel surface. Soon there is a clear view (left) of Kew Palace.

STRAND-ON-THE-GREEN was just a cluster of fishermen's cottages until 1770. Painter John Zoffany lived at Zoffany House (the blue plaque can just be seen) from 1780 to 1810 and modelled the Disciples in his 'Last Supper' on local fishermen. The Lord Mayor of London's barge used to be laid up in front of The City Barge (near the railway bridge) which dates from 1484.

KEW GREEN. The church was built in 1714 and dedicated to St Anne after Queen Anne had given the site and £100 towards the costs. Queen Mary's parents were married here after the Duke of Teck had proposed in Kew Gardens. The Mausoleum at the east end of the church held the remains of Queen Mary's grandparents, the Duke and Duchess of Cambridge (who lived at the porticoed Cambridge Cottage), until they were removed to Windsor in 1930. The first Duke of Cambridge's excessive participation in services here led one curate to resign. (Curate: 'Let us pray'; Duke: 'By all means.') Gainsborough, the painter, is buried outside the south wall whilst Zoffany's tomb is to the east of the church. Archbishop Lang, who was involved in the King Edward VIII abdication crisis, retired to King's Cottage (by the church) where he died. Jo Grimond lived at number 71 (north side) when he was leader of the Liberal Party. The teashops have now disappeared from the Green but in nearby Kew Road there is the Maids of Honour teashop where are baked, according to a secret recipe, the Maids of Honour cakes as made for Henry VIII at Richmond (the teashop is open daily until 5.30pm, except on Sundays and Monday afternoons).

KEW PALACE was built in 1631 by a Dutchman. Later it was an annexe to a larger and now demolished Royal home. In 1802 George III moved into the house and his wife, Queen Charlotte, died here in 1818 four months after Queen Victoria's parents were married in the drawing room. The interior has been carefully restored and includes portraits by Zoffany. The garden was laid out only in 1969 as the back of the house had originally been subject to flooding. The mount, peeping over the wall, was inspired by the tradition of providing a view from enclosed gardens. The Palace (reached by way of Kew Gardens) is open daily from 11.00am to 5.30pm (2.00 to 6.00pm on Sundays) from April to September; admission is 60p, children and pensioners 30p.

Thames towpath at Kew

There is a view (half right) of the wide entrance to the Grand Union Canal and then the Kew Gardens' Brentford Gate (left).

THE ROYAL BOTANIC GARDENS, known as Kew Gardens, were founded about 1759 by Princess Augusta, George III's mother. The Orangery was her greenhouse and during her son's reign his next-door Richmond estate was amalgamated with the Kew Gardens. William Cobbett, the writer and radical MP, was a garden-boy here during this period. The Pagoda, built for the Princess in 1761, was decorated with eighty dragons until the Prince Regent pawned them to pay his debts. In the centre of the Temperate House, one of the largest greenhouses in the world, is a Chilean Hairy Palm which was grown from seed in 1843, whilst the Palm House has a plant dating from 1775. The Aroid House, designed by John Nash, once stood at the back of Buckingham Palace as its twin still does. There is a tea bar near the Brentford Gate, open until 7.00pm (3.00pm in winter). The 300-acre gardens are open daily from 10.00am to dusk; admission 15p.

Syon House

SYON HOUSE. The view from the river was painted by George III. A monastery was on the site of the house before the Reformation and one of its members, St Richard Reynolds, was hanged for refusing to recognise Henry VIII as head of the Church. Apart from a brief return under Mary I, the female section of the community went abroad and today the convent is in Devon. In 1547 Charles I, who was being held at Hampton Court, was allowed to sail downstream to visit his family at Syon. The Earl of Northumberland received the estate from James I and today Syon is the home of the Duke of Northumberland. The lion, the family crest, can be seen on the roof — this same lion once stood on Northumberland House which was demolished in the nineteenth century to make way for Northumberland Avenue, off Trafalgar Square. The conservatory (to the right) inspired Paxton's Crystal Palace.

After nearly ½ mile the trees (left) fall away to give a view into Kew Gardens. The break in the trees was planned to provide a view from the Gardens across the river to Syon House.

The path becomes enclosed by trees and just before the towpath bears south there is a view across the water to Syon Pavilion and Isleworth.

Soon the still wooded path becomes metalled and passes Richmond Lock. On approaching Twickenham Bridge (erected only in 1933) there is a glimpse (left) over the Old Deer Park to the Pagoda in Kew Gardens. Continue under the Richmond Railway Bridge (opened in 1848 and designed by Locke who was also responsible for Barnes Bridge) and turn left, before Asgill House, to walk up Old Palace Lane.

Syon Pavilion

99

Isleworth

Beyond The White Swan (left) turn right into Old Palace Yard where a public footpath runs across a courtyard and under the gateway of Richmond Palace to reach Richmond Green. To reach Richmond Station follow the metalled path across the Green, keep right at a junction of paths and walk up Duke Street. Turn left for the station.

ISLEWORTH. The attractive Syon Pavilion, a Tudor boathouse converted during the Georgian period as a tea-house, is now a private residence. Isleworth Church is modern apart from a fifteenth-century tower. The bodies of many Great Plague victims were brought here by barge for burial in 1665. Both Turner and Van Gogh lived in the village. The local pub is called The London Apprentice since apprentices of the livery companies used to row up the river from London on their annual day off.

RICHMOND would still have been known as West Sheen had not Henry VII called his palace here Richmond Palace after one of his titles, Earl of Richmond, derived from Richmond in Yorkshire. Henry VIII often visited with Catherine of Aragon. Shakespeare stayed in the town when his players performed for Elizabeth I, who also spent much time here. The Queen died at the palace in 1603 and Sir Robert Carey at once rode from the palace gateway to tell King James in Edinburgh that he was also King of England. Charles I was the last monarch to live here, the building being badly damaged after his execution. The Bishop Duppa Almshouses in The Vineyard were founded by Charles I's chaplain who lived in Richmond during the Interregnum. Maids of Honour Row on the Green was built in 1724 to house ladies-in-waiting to the Princess of Wales (the future George II's Queen Caroline) who was living at (the now demolished) Richmond Lodge in the Old Deer Park.

Henry VII gave £10 towards rebuilding the parish church and traces of Tudor work remain. On the north wall there is a memorial to Robert Cotton who was an Officer of the Wardrobe under both Mary I and Elizabeth I. A new floor slab indicates the position of actor Edmund Kean's tomb — he spent his last two years in Richmond and may have been refused burial in Westminster Abbey due to his excessive drinking habits. T. S. Eliot and Dorothy L. Sayers were once members of the recently restored St John's Church, near the station, and Richard Dimbleby used to play the organ at St Matthias up the hill. Marion Evans first used the pseudonym George Eliot whilst living in Parkshot (on the site of the magistrate's court) where she wrote part of *Scenes of Clerical Life*. The Hogarth Press was founded on the kitchen table at Hogarth House in Paradise Street when Leonard and Virginia Woolf were living there during the First World War. Café Mozart in Church Court is open daily but closes early on Sunday afternoons. Mrs Beeton's on Hill Rise is open daily until 5.00pm.

Walk 11
RICHMOND HILL

Richmond — Petersham — Ham —
Richmond Park — Richmond

5-mile circular walk   OS sheet 176

Although this is a short walk, plenty of time should be allowed for looking at the views from the river, Richmond Park and Richmond Hill. The route continues the Putney–Richmond towpath walk (Walk 10) before turning into the Park which, with its unfenced roads and deer, can sometimes resemble Scotland.

Richmond is at the end of the London Transport District Line and can also be reached by British Rail trains from

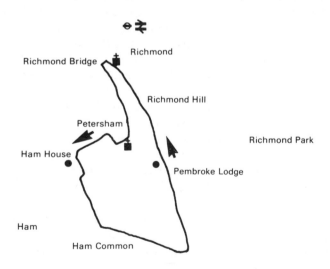

Walk 11 **RICHMOND HILL**

Richmond Palace Gate

Waterloo. Red Buses 65 and 71 run between Richmond and Kingston via Ham.

RICHMOND (see Walk 10)

At Richmond Bridge (built in 1777) descend to the towpath by the steps on either side of the road and turn left to walk upstream. Beyond The Three Pigeons (left) the path is separated from the river by a lawn.

On reaching a T-junction go ahead through a turnstile to follow a metalled path across Petersham Meadows. Beyond barriers the way becomes enclosed and meets a lane at a bend on the edge of Petersham village.

To visit the church go ahead; the Walk continues to the right.

Where the lane ends, keep forward along a narrow passage to River Lane. Turn right to pass eighteenth-century Petersham

Lodge (left) and the empty cowsheds (right). Where the lane runs into the Thames, turn left along the towpath. After 400 yards the eighteenth-century Marble Hill House can be seen between the trees on the far bank.

After a few yards leave the towpath by turning left on to a short concrete path. The way then bears half right over grass

Indian Balsam, found on the towpath

PETERSHAM. The church tower is seventeenth-century but the chancel is partly Norman, and from the Georgian box pews it is impossible for the congregation to see the altar. This tiny church is now used again for the main Sunday service, since the Italianate All Saints' Church in Bute Avenue has proved too expensive to heat. Famous weddings which took place here include the Lauderdales in 1672 (*see page 105*) and the Queen Mother's parents in 1881. George Vancouver, the discoverer of Vancouver Island who lived at Navigator's Cottage in River Lane, is buried by the churchyard's south wall. Charles Dickens wrote part of *Nicholas Nickleby* at Elm Lodge (near Sudbrook Lane) in Petersham Road. Until the 1970s cows were still milked at the Express Dairy's River Lane Farm.

beside a wire fence (left) to join a metalled path at a corner, which leads to Ham House.

Take the metalled path along the east side of Ham House; there is a glimpse of the garden at a break in the wall (right). At the end of the path turn right on to a grass path which, at a sharp bend, affords another view of the Ham House garden. After the bend, the path (the old south drive) runs straight ahead for ½ mile to Ham Common. On the way the long avenue crosses Sandy Lane.

Turn right here for bus stops and then left to pass Cardinal Newman's house (see page 106) and find a café (closed Sundays).

HAM HOUSE was built in 1610 for Sir Thomas Vavasour and inherited by Elizabeth Dysart who, as a friend of Oliver Cromwell, saved the royalist Earl of Lauderdale (*see page 21*) from execution. In 1672 Elizabeth married Lauderdale (the 'L' in Charles II's Cabal) in Petersham Church just six months after his first wife had died. Charles II gave them a dukedom as a wedding present and the couple set about lavishly decorating the house; it has been preserved almost intact — even the kitchen still has its original dresser and table as well as seventeenth-century gadgets. The garden, laid out like a Union Jack, has recently been restored and is maturing. In 1678 John Evelyn wrote that Ham 'is indeed inferior to few of the best villas in Italy itself; the House furnished like a great Prince's; the park with Flower Gardens, Orangeries, Groves, Avenues, Courts, Statues, Perspectives, Fountains, Aviaries and all this at the banks of the sweetest River in the World, must needs be admired'. Later Horace Walpole wrote: 'It is so blocked up and barricaded with walls, vast trees, and gates, that you think yourself a hundred miles off and a hundred years back . . .' The house is open daily except Mondays from 2.00 to 6.00pm (12 noon to 4.00pm October to March); admission 50p, pensioners and children 20p. There is no charge for visiting the garden, where teas are served during the summer.

Ham House

HAM. The Prince Regent and Mrs Fitzherbert spent part
of their honeymoon at Ormeley Lodge (*see page 107*) on the
north-east side of the Common. Beverley Nichols, who lives
at nearby Sudbrook Cottage, opens his famous garden on
Sunday afternoons in May. The Queen Mother's mother,
before her wedding at Petersham (*see page 104*), lived at
Forbes House (now rebuilt) on the west side of the
Common, while the Queen Mother's sister, Violet
Hyacinth Bowes-Lyon who died aged 11 (before the Queen
Mother's birth), is buried in St Andrew's churchyard (west
side opposite the lychgate) which is on the south-west side
of the Common. Cardinal Newman spent part of his
childhood at Newman House (part of the school) in Ham
Street where, in 1805, he saw the windows illuminated
with candles to celebrate the victory at Trafalgar. The
Cardinal later claimed that when he dreamt of heaven he
dreamt of Ham.

On reaching the gateway at Ham Common turn left along the road and at Nightingales Close (left) bear half right with the main traffic to approach a crossroads by a bus stop near The New Inn (left).

Cross the road and walk ahead up the left-hand side of Ham Gate Avenue. Soon the roadside path passes Sudbrook Cottage and Ormeley Lodge (left). (St Andrew's is beyond the trees on the right.) After just over ½ mile the road enters Richmond Park at Ham Gate just beyond Park Gate House.

Keep ahead on the metalled path by the Park road. Soon the path becomes rough and begins to rise above the road. As soon as the way is level, with a pond to the right, turn left up a narrow path which climbs up to pass under an oak tree. The long path ahead, known as Hornbeam Walk, continues on along the edge of the hill. At one point the path goes over a steep hump by a tree.

On approaching the grounds of Pembroke Lodge the path merges with another from the right. The way then follows the boundary fence (left) to the Lodge. The house can be reached through a gate by the toilets (left).

RICHMOND PARK. Charles I enclosed Shene Chase in 1637 and now the deer and the unfenced roads bring a feeling of Scotland to Surrey. There are believed to be over 600 red and fallow deer living in the Park; about 100 are culled each year under a Royal Venison Warrant signed by the Queen. The Archbishop of Canterbury, the Prime Minister and other eminent people are entitled to receive a quarter of venison each whilst the Lord Mayor of London can claim four quarters to maintain his table. White Lodge (now the Royal Ballet School), in the centre of the Park, was built in 1728 for George II. Queen Mary spent part of her childhood at this house, where later her son, the Duke of Windsor, was born and baptised in 1894. Princess Alexandra lives to the south-west at Thatched House Lodge, once the home of Sir Robert Walpole, the first British Prime Minister. Refreshments can be obtained at Pembroke Lodge (*see page 108*).

After crossing the main driveway entrance to the Lodge the path becomes metalled and moves farther away from the road (right). To the left behind a fence, there is Henry VIII's Mound — one of the many places where the King is said to have watched for a signal from the Tower of London confirming Anne Boleyn's execution. After ¼ mile the path reaches Richmond Gate at the top of Star and Garter Hill.

Logs in Richmond Park

PEMBROKE LODGE was originally a small building known as Molecatcher's Cottage. In the eighteenth century it was greatly enlarged for Elizabeth, Countess of Pembroke, who died here aged 93 in 1831. The Lodge was then the home of Elizabeth Fitzclarence, the daughter of William IV by the actress Mrs Jordan. In 1847 Queen Victoria gave the house to her Prime Minister Lord John Russell who also enlarged the building. His grandson, Bertrand Russell, spent much of his childhood here. The tearoom on the ground floor is open daily until 6.00pm during the summer, and winter weekends. There are magnificent views across Ham from the terrace at the back of the house where you can also take coffee or meals.

Toadstool

Go ahead to pass the front of the Star & Garter Home (left) and reach the Richmond Hill viewpoint beyond Nightingale Lane.

To reach the centre of Richmond continue downhill past the viewpoint. For part of the way there is a parallel path along the top of Terrace Gardens (left). Mrs Beeton's (open until 5.00pm for tea) is on the right near the bottom of the hill.

RICHMOND HILL. Richmond in Virginia took its name from this landmark after a tobacco farmer standing here was reminded of a similar view of the James River. The scene below has been reproduced by many artists including George Barret Junior, J. H. Muntz, Peter de Wint, Antonio Joli, Turner and Walter Sickert. Sir John Mills and his theatrical family lived at The Wick on the corner of Nightingale Lane, whilst Sir Joshua Reynolds lived for twenty years, on and off, at Wick House next door until his death there in 1792. The huge Star & Garter Home for Disabled Soldiers, Sailors and Airmen stands on the site of the Star & Garter Hotel where Charles Dickens often stayed.

Walk 12
WINDSOR GREAT PARK

*Windsor — Datchet — Old Windsor — Runnymede
— Windsor Great Park — Windsor*

10- or 11½-mile circular walk   OS sheet 176

The creation of Windsor Great Park began in 1086 when William the Conqueror enclosed an area of woodland. The Castle and Park were separate until Charles II's time. George III personally supervised the staking out of roads and in 1790 he appointed himself Ranger. Queen Victoria was greatly attached to the Park and with Prince Albert made many improvements. A model village for Royal staff was built in 1948 by George VI. The deer, which had been here since the Norman period, were removed when the 1939 war effort required more farming activity, and were re-introduced, from Balmoral and Richmond, only in 1979.

This circular Walk uses the Thames towpath and the Great Park's paths. Those daunted by the prospect of an 11½-mile walk can save 1½ miles by starting at Datchet where there is a station on British Rail's Southern Region Waterloo—Windsor line. Walkers will want to rest at the Copper Horse Statue to enjoy the view; the last 2½ miles can be easy as you simply walk in a straight line towards the Castle which is always in view. If the Walk is to be divided into two outings, Runnymede (4½ miles) can be treated as a half-way point. Buses run across the meadow and at the south end there is Egham with a British Rail station on the Waterloo—Reading line. There is no food on sale inside the Great Park except during the summer in The Savill Garden; an admission ticket must be purchased (*see page 117*).

Windsor has two railway stations. The Paddington line trains meet the Windsor trains at Slough; the Southern Region

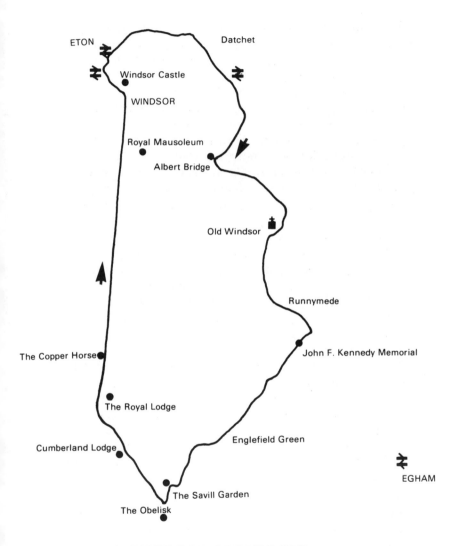

Walk 12 **WINDSOR GREAT PARK**

trains run from Waterloo and stop at Staines. The Green Line
runs a non-stop coach (Route 700) from Victoria Coach Station
during the summer. Green Line 718 and 724 serve Old Windsor
and Englefield Green.

The Walk starts at the Windsor and Eton Riverside Station.
Go along Datchet Road to pass the side (left) of the station and
the former Royal Waiting Room. Keep to the pavement on the
left side as the road becomes Edward VII Avenue and runs
through the only public part of The Home Park.

After crossing Victoria Bridge over the Thames, continue for
only a few yards before turning left through a wide gap in the
hedge. Ignore the 'Datchet Golf Club Private' notice and at
once go right to follow a footpath which runs parallel to the
road (right). The way is over grass and when the open space
narrows into a track do not swing to the left with the track
but go ahead on a narrow path through trees and bushes. Soon

WINDSOR. William the Conqueror built the first fortress
here and the oldest parts of the present castle date from
Henry II. The castle was restored for George IV by Sir
Jeffry Wyatville who achieved the present silhouette. Soon
after, Queen Victoria came here and fell in love with
Albert. Queen Elizabeth II spends most weekends here as
well as Christmas and Easter. The Guildhall in the High
Street was designed by Christopher Wren and completed
in 1690 when the Council insisted on pillars being added as
the building looked unsafe — however the extra pillars do
not touch the ceiling. J. S. Stone wrote the hymn 'The
Church's One Foundation' whilst serving as curate at the
parish church next door. The church building dates only
from 1820 but it contains a painting of 'The Last Supper'
by Franz de Cleyn which George III had moved from St
George's Chapel. H. G. Wells worked as a draper's
assistant in a shop now occupied by Token House and the
Midland Bank in the High Street. There are several
teashops in the lanes off Castle Hill, by the entrance to the
castle precincts, which are open daily; admission to the
castle precincts is free.

Windsor Guildhall

the way joins the road again by the first house (Sumpter Mead) in Datchet. Continue along the road to pass the end of the High Street (left) where there is a fine view over the river (right).

DATCHET. The Victorian church has a partly thirteenth-century chancel and the east window is a copy of the original church's fourteenth-century window. There are Tudor brasses and Charles II's Royal Arms are above the south door. Until the building of the Victoria and Albert Bridge in the mid-nineteenth century the High Street was linked — by ferry and then a bridge — to the tree-lined lane on the far bank, which features in Shakespeare's *The Merry Wives of Windsor*. Group Captain Peter Townsend, George VI's equerry, lived at Adelaide Cottage, next to the grey castillated Adelaide Lodge which can also be seen across the water (*see page 119*).

The pavement continues beyond the village and gives way to a wide grass verge. Beyond a short stretch of old road there is again a metalled footpath and, on approaching Southlea Farm, a clear view of the Copper Horse ahead (*see page 120*). The path continues as a pavement to Albert Bridge. Cross the bridge, which affords views of the Prince Consort's Home Farm and the castle (right), and turn left down a flight of steps to join the towpath.

The riverside path runs through grass and crosses a stream which flows from Windsor Great Park. On coming level with the weir (left) there is another view of the Copper Horse (right). The towpath, which follows the New Cut rather than the old channel, enjoys a grass surface as far as the Ham Lane bridge (left). Cross the lane and follow the now metalled towpath. Beyond the Old Windsor Lock (at the end of the cut) the path narrows. After crossing a steep concrete bridge the way becomes rough. Where the bank is subject to erosion the path now runs behind a line of trees (left). Soon there is a gravel surface before the path crosses a high concrete bridge over an inlet. The enclosed footpath on the right leads to Old Windsor Church.

The towpath turns sharply left and has various surfaces as the way passes riverside gardens. After ¼ mile the towpath passes the Little Chef café before running through a boatyard.

OLD WINDSOR CHURCH is the only church dedicated to both St Peter and St Andrew. Old Windsor was the original town where both Edward the Confessor and William I came before Windsor Castle was built' some 3 miles away. It was here that an Ecclesiastical Council decided in 1072 that the Archbishop of York owed canonical obedience to Canterbury. The church has a thirteenth-century tower and chancel. In the churchyard (by the tiny north-east gate) there is the tomb of Mary Robinson whose portraits by Gainsborough, Romney and Reynolds can be seen in the Wallace Collection. The church is open daily from 2.00 to 4.30pm during the summer (from Easter to Harvest Festival).

The path continues just below the main road (right). (Go up the steps to reach bus stops and The Bells of Ouseley.) After a short distance the path joins the road. The pavement stays by the river (left) when the road continues ahead. The towpath becomes uneven and, after passing a Victorian boathouse, goes on to Runnymede.

Continue ahead by the river and, on coming level with the stone house on the far bank, turn away from the water to cross the road and follow a faint path across the meadow towards the trees on the side of Cooper's Hill.

To reach Egham (1 mile) turn left after crossing the road and keep forward where the road swings away.

On reaching a wooden kissing gate in the trees go ahead up the cobbled woodland path. This is part of the Kennedy memorial and the path becomes stepped before reaching the block of Portland Stone.

RUNNYMEDE. The Magna Carta Memorial (west side) was erected by the American Bar Association in 1957 and recalls that somewhere on this wide green area in 1215 King John agreed to the 63 clauses of Magna Carta. This document, described as 'the first ground and chief cornerstone of the common law of England' was the first attempt to express in legal terms some of the leading ideas of constitutional government. One of the two lodges, designed in 1930 by Sir Edwin Lutyens, is a tearoom which opens from 10.00am to 6.00pm from Easter to October.

JOHN F. KENNEDY MEMORIAL. In 1965 the Queen came here and handed over three acres of meadow and woodland to the USA as a memorial to President Kennedy. The land was received by Secretary of State Dean Rusk in the presence of Mrs Jacqueline Kennedy, Robert Kennedy and John Kennedy. Carved on the seven-ton block of Portland stone is a quotation from the Declaration of Freedom included in President Kennedy's inaugural address.

Keep to the left of the Kennedy stone and follow the path which loses its cobbled surface and bends to climb the hill. After following a wooden fence (left) the way joins a metalled drive known as Oak Lane. Beyond a further junction there is part of Brunel University's Shoreditch campus (left). The lane runs uphill through trees to meet Priest Hill.

Cross the road and turn left to walk uphill. From here there is a view north to the Queen Mother Reservoir at Sunnymeads. At the top of the hill pass the bus shelter and turn right into Castle Hill Road which runs through a wood on the edge of Englefield Green.

Milestone

On reaching Bishopsgate Road keep ahead down Ham Lane. After 150 yards the metalled surface ends as the lane continues along the side of fields (right). Just before reaching a red brick cottage turn left to go over an iron stile and enter a field at a corner. Go ahead along the edge of the field by a wood (right). At the far end go over another stile and into a second field. Keep ahead by the side (right) of the field as the way runs downhill. Before reaching the dip go over a stile and down a few concrete steps to follow an enclosed path. The narrow way joins the end of Prospect Lane. Walk down the unmade lane to pass several cottages and reach Wick Lane near The Sun.

Turn left to pass the top of King's Lane and the pub (left). Follow Wick Lane for ¼ mile before turning right into the Savill Garden car park where there are excellent toilets. Go through a wooden gateway to enter Windsor Great Park and follow a short metalled path to a T-junction opposite the Savill Garden entrance.

Turn left on to a wide Park road (part of the Rhododendron Walk) to reach The Obelisk.

THE SAVILL GARDEN. Sir Eric Savill began to create this garden in 1932 after he became Deputy Surveyor of Windsor Great Park. The 35 acres of woodland were then covered with rhododendron bushes which had been planted as game coverts. George V and Queen Mary encouraged the work in what was at that time called the Bog Garden. George VI changed the name to the Savill Garden. It is known as a garden for all seasons and there is a range of camellias, magnolias, hydrangeas as well as a great variety of other shrubs together with trees. Sir Eric lived nearby until his death in 1980. The garden is open daily from 10.00am to 7.00pm (or sunset if earlier) from 1st March to Christmas Eve; admission is £1, pensioners and children 85p. Refreshments are available inside the garden during the summer.

THE OBELISK was erected by George II to commemorate the success of his son, the Duke of Cumberland, at the Battle of Culloden in 1746 when he put down the last Jacobite rebellion. The nearby Obelisk Pond and Virginia Water were dug in order to create work for Cumberland's army which had been raised to fight the supporters of Bonnie Prince Charlie.

Bear right to leave the metalled surface and pass The Obelisk (left). Keep turning right with the fence (right) to walk down a sandy path which crosses Stone Bridge and the end of Obelisk Pond. Continue ahead up the very wide grassed Obelisk Ride. The Savill Garden is on the right and Smith's Lawn (the polo ground) is to the left where the equestrian statue of Prince Albert can be seen on the far side.

Cumberland Obelisk

On reaching a junction of paths at Cumberland Gate, go ahead over a road to pass the gate (right), pass a short hedge (right) and find a riding track. Turn right on to the track and after a few yards take the left fork — a sandy track. Keep on the track which narrows and, after ¼ mile, crosses the metalled avenue leading to Cumberland Lodge (left).

Keep forward to pass a tennis court (left). The path becomes less defined as it runs over grass to reach a road near a junction of Park roads by the Chaplain's Lodge (left). Go ahead across the road to follow the wooden fence (right) of the densely wooded Royal Lodge Grounds. The path becomes more defined as the way runs downhill. Where the fence curves away keep ahead on the path which, after Ox Pond (left), becomes a wide hedged grassway. Ahead on the hill is the Copper Horse statue and soon there is a view (right) of the pink Royal Lodge.

CUMBERLAND LODGE was built by Charles II and for many years was the official home of the Great Park's Ranger. The house, now a conference and study centre, takes its name from the Duke of Cumberland who became Ranger after the Battle of Culloden and enlarged the building. Earlier the first Duke of Marlborough had died here when his wife was the Ranger. After a fire in 1811 Sir Jeffry Wyatville rebuilt the house which was again altered after a second fire in 1869. The clock (which is not always correct) dates from Cumberland's period here.

ROYAL LODGE is the Queen Mother's weekend home. The original house was called Lower Lodge when Thomas Sandby, the architect who assisted Cumberland, lived here in the eighteenth century. The name was changed to King's Cottage for the Prince Regent who engaged John Nash to make improvements. William IV demolished most of this building and used some of the materials to erect Adelaide Cottage (*see page 113*) in The Home Park. George V gave the remains of the house to his son, the Duke of York (and future George VI) who added wings and had the new house painted pink to remind the Duchess (now the Queen Mother) of her childhood home, St Paul's Waldenbury. Royal Lodge was the childhood home of the Queen and Princess Margaret and here their parents spent a long weekend during the Abdication crisis waiting for a call from King Edward VIII (later Duke of Windsor) at nearby Fort Belvedere. The chapel in the grounds was rebuilt by Queen Victoria.

The Copper Horse

THE COPPER HORSE stands on Snow Hill, once known as Snowdon, which affords a magnificent view down the Long Walk to Windsor Castle (*see page 112*). Slough can be seen beyond and the Queen Mother Reservoir to the east. The 2½-mile Long Walk was created for Charles II and lined by rows of elms which have now been replaced by London plane and horse chestnut trees. George IV laid the foundation stone for the Copper Horse in 1829 in the presence of the sculptor, Sir Richard Westmacott, and Sir Jeffry Wyatville. The horse, which has George III in Roman costume mounted on its back, was hoisted into position in 1831 when a furnace had to be set up here to repair one of the legs which had broken. On the eve of Jubilee Day 1977 the Queen came here to light the first of a nationwide chain of celebratory bonfires.

At the end of the wide path go through the gate in the deer fence and walk ahead to the Copper Horse statue.

Beyond the statue walk down the hill to go the length of the Long Walk below. At the double gates by the lodge go through the kissing gate on the left. After the Walk has crossed a main road, there is a view (right) of the Royal Mausoleum.

On reaching the gates below Windsor Castle turn left to leave the Long Walk and enter Park Street which leads into Windsor's High Street.

The Long Walk leading to Windsor Castle

THE ROYAL MAUSOLEUM was built in 1862 to house the body of the Prince Consort who had died suddenly the previous year. The building, based on a mausoleum at Coburg, is built in the thirteenth-century Italian style. Queen Victoria arranged for her own body to be brought here on her death and it is now traditional for members of the Royal Family to be buried in the garden outside the building. The Mausoleum can be visited on the Wednesday nearest Queen Victoria's birthday, 24 May.

Walk 13
THE COLNE VALLEY

Langley — Langley Park — Iver — Langley

9-mile circular walk   OS sheet 176

Many believed Coppins, Princess Marina's Buckinghamshire
home, to be deep in the Chilterns. It is, in fact, within a short
walking distance of the London borough of Hillingdon. Until
recently the countryside here was in danger of being squeezed
by Uxbridge in the east, Slough to the south-west and mineral
workings in the north. Artist Paul Nash, who lived here,
described it as 'real country, only 15 miles from London'. Now
the Colne Valley Park, which stretches from Rickmansworth
to Staines, encompasses this area and, with the assistance of
the GLC, seeks to preserve and enhance the natural environ-

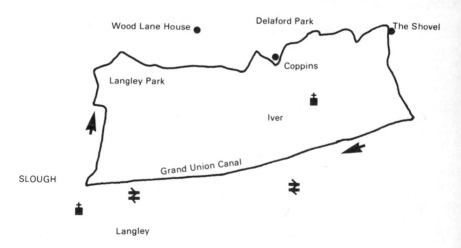

Walk 13 **THE COLNE VALLEY**

122

Langley Church

ment. This circular Walk passes through Langley Park and royal Iver before returning by way of the Grand Union Canal (built in 1795) and its Slough branch which has several aqueducts.

Langley Station is on the British Rail's Paddington–Slough line and can be reached quickly from central London. The Walk may be left off or taken up at the end of Iver Lane which is linked to Uxbridge Underground Station (Metropolitan and Piccadilly Lines) by Red Buses 222 and 224.

Leave Langley Station, which has a large car park, by the 'up' platform where the Victorian station building stands and walk north along Langley Park Road. Turn right into Canal Wharf to reach the Slough branch of the Grand Union Canal. Turn left to walk under the road with the water on the right.

After just over ¼ mile there is a view (half left) of Langley Church. Walk up on to the footbridge. *Turn left only to view the church — the footpath runs across a road junction to pass the seventeenth-century almshouses.*

LANGLEY CHURCH is also known as Langley Marish Church after the de Marisco family who held the manor under Edward I. This church has been described as one of the most rewarding in Buckinghamshire (although in 1974 it became part of Berkshire). Although there are traces of the Norman building, the church is now largely twelfth-century with an early seventeenth-century tower. The porch is fifteenth-century. To the left of the high altar is the Kedermister monument. The unusual library in the church, often consulted by John Milton, was founded in 1623 by Sir John Kedermister of Langley Park. Paul Nash, the painter who designed the moquette upholstery for London bus seats (as well as book-jackets, rugs, stage sets, ceramics, glassware and posters) often attended Sunday morning service here as a child in the 1890s. His grandfather lived in Westmoor House at George Green and Paul particularly enjoyed riding to church in the dog cart with his grandfather whilst people waved at them. He recalled that the 'inside of the church was so enthralling that it was difficult to keep up an appearance of interest in the service. From the family pew in the choir, I had a view of the congregation beyond the screen and of the exquisite little chain library on the far wall. More constantly my eyes strayed to the clear glass east window where the branches of trees showed through, or to the lovely painted vault above, pale, clear blue painted with golden stars and bunches of corn.' (The corn was probably the sheaf on the hatchment.) Paul Nash and his wife, Margaret, are buried at the side of the walled Harvey grave behind the Hall. His great-grandfather, who lived at (now demolished) Langley Hall, once turned George II off the estate when the royal party passed over from Windsor. Queen Elizabeth the Queen Mother is a collector of Paul Nash paintings. The Red Lion opposite the church is sixteenth-century and has a garden at the back.

Paul Nash's tomb

The Walk continues across the canal footbridge. A narrow gravel path runs downhill to give a view over a lake (left). Do not go ahead towards the pylon but bear half right on a narrow path which runs along the bottom of a bank (left). Beyond a stream the way is across grass and along a short metalled path

Langley Park Lodge

Langley Park

running between temporary homes and caravans. The path joins a road. Ignore the junctions and go ahead where the road bears left. Cross a wooden stile by a gate and keep straight on through an orchard.

At the far end cross another stile and still keep forward across open land. In the winter there is an early glimpse of the mansion in Langley Park. On the far side go over a wooden stile and turn left for 200 yards. Soon after crossing a stream climb over a stile on the right. The path follows a wire fence (right) and then a lake (right). Across the water there is Langley Park's eighteenth-century mansion.

LANGLEY PARK was owned by Edward VI but Charles I gave the estate to Sir John Kedermister (*see page 124*). The present house was built in 1738 for the third Duke of Marlborough who thought his grandfather's Blenheim Palace to be too far from London. The Harvey family bought the Park in 1788 and the mansion is now owned by Buckinghamshire County Council.

At the top end of the lake go through a double kissing gate (by an old iron gate) and follow the path which bears eastwards. The way crosses the impressive tree-lined driveway. On approaching the stables bear left round a wooden gate. The gravel path passes the arboretum (right). Where the way divides go right with the fence (right) and follow the path for ¼ mile. Walk between wooden barriers at the side of a gate and go ahead along a narrow path to emerge at Ashen Cross.

Walk ahead up Bellswood Lane to reach, after just over ¼ mile, Wood Lane. *Wood Lane House is ¼ mile to the right.*

The Walk continues across the road from Bellswood Lane where there is a wooden stile some yards to the right of the gate. Cross the stile and follow the hedge (right) along the side of a field. At another stile the hedge gives way to a wire fence. Cross a third stile and follow a new metalled path to reach Love Green beyond a stile by a gate.

Turn right for a few yards and then bear half left to cross the road and go over a drive to a house on the corner. Follow the garden (left) to a stile in the iron fence opposite Roger Motor Services. Turn left to walk up Love Green Lane. There is a rustic cottage ahead. At the junction with Bangors Road South (where there is a seat) cross the road and turn right. Soon the pavement passes the entrance to Coppins.

WOOD LANE HOUSE was built in 1901 for the Nash family when Paul was 12 years old. From here he travelled to his evening classes in Bolt Court, off Fleet Street, and was often moved by the shapes and shadows he observed when cycling home from Uxbridge Station. He made a drawing of The Colne (*see page 129*) and other works include 'Landscape at Wood Lane', and 'Tree Group, Iver Heath'. 'Bird Garden', now in Cardiff's National Museum of Wales, shows part of the garden in 1911. The following year he staged his first exhibition, thanks to an introduction to Sir William Richmond from a local resident. Wood Lane House was also the childhood home of Paul's brother, John, and their works hang together in the Imperial War Museum.

127

At the corner of Coppins turn left into Coppins Lane whilst the main road continues into Iver.

The Walk continues up Coppins Lane at the side of the

COPPINS. The Copyns family lived in a house on this site in the Middle Ages. The present nineteenth-century building was erected for John Mitchell who arranged theatre visits for Queen Victoria and later Edward VI. The house was later the home of a lady-in-waiting before Queen Victoria's grand-daughter, Princess Victoria, moved here. In 1935 Coppins passed to the Duke of Kent who had just married Princess Marina. He brought his collection of clocks and antiques, and from here vegetables and flowers from the garden were sent up to the couple's Belgrave Square house. The Queen, Princess Margaret and Prince Philip came here as children. Other visitors included Queen Mary, Princess Juliana of the Netherlands, Mrs Simpson (who later became the Duchess of Windsor) in 1936, Sir Winston Churchill and General Smuts. The Princess, with her daughter Princess Alexandra, continued to live here after her husband was killed on active service in 1942 and only moved to Kensington when her son, the present Duke of Kent, married in 1961. Since he sold the property in 1972, a new owner has removed part of the high wall to give a better view of the house.

IVER was called Evreham in the Domesday Book. The church dates from the Saxon period when the builders used some Roman bricks. The thirteenth-century nave pillars are supporting some Norman arches on the north side. The eighteenth-century Bridgefoot House, recently the home of architect G. F. Bodley (*see page 39*), was the dower house of (the now demolished) Huntsmoor Park house where Samuel Pepys, John Evelyn and Alexander Pope stayed. The Swan is sixteenth-century. Iver Station (closed on Sundays), on the Paddington line, is ¾ mile to the south of the church.

Bridgefoot House at Iver

former royal home. After a glimpse of the garden (left) and a group of houses (right) the lane bears right and loses its metalled surface. The way runs gently downhill between fields with a view (half left) over Uxbridge. Beyond a wooden stile by a gate the path runs unfenced ahead under trees through Delaford Park. On approaching Colne Brook the path bears right in front of two residences and crosses the water.

The drive turns right with the water and then left to go through a white gate. Go round another bend to pass Daffodil Cottage (left) — do not go through the double iron gates. The lane, now known as Palmer's Moor Lane, passes several houses before turning south on a metalled surface to meet Iver Lane.

Turn left along Iver Lane to cross the River Colne and enter Hillingdon. Continue ahead to a second bridge which spans the Grand Union Canal. *For buses to Uxbridge continue ahead and turn right at The Coachman's Inn.*

The Walk continues to The Shovel by the canal. Walk past the pub (left) to follow the towpath which crosses Fray's River and passes a lock. There is usually a large number of barges moored between the lock and the Benbow Waye bridge ahead.

Just beyond the new bridge at Packet Boat Lane the towpath crosses an old bridge over the entrance to a wharf. The wine bar opposite is open every lunchtime except Saturdays and welcomes children for Sunday lunch.

After 400 yards cross the iron footbridge to leave the Uxbridge–Brentford Canal and follow the Slough branch. The first of several aqueducts crosses Fray's River. Later, after passing under an iron bridge, the canal crosses the River Colne which gives its name to this regional park. Soon after crossing the Colne Brook the towpath approaches a brick bridge. Leave the water to walk up a slope to the bridge. Do not cross the bridge but continue ahead along Court Lane above the canal (right). Across the water there are views of Iver church. The metalled lane meets Thorney Lane. *For Iver Station (closed on Sundays) turn left.*

The Walk continues ahead along the top of the high bank. At first the way is open but after nearly ½ mile there is a long high fence to the left. After a wide footbridge the path rejoins the water; the surface here is uneven. The canal narrows briefly at the site of a demolished bridge and then passes the only unsightly area — a dump and a caravan park (left). Beyond a further bridge the towpath passes a boatyard (right) before reaching Canal Wharf near the next bridge.

Walk up Canal Wharf and turn left along Langley Park Road to reach Langley Station.

130

Walk 14
THE CHILTERN HILLS
Amersham — Chalfont St Giles — Chorleywood

7½ miles   OS sheet 176

The Metropolitan Line from Baker Street reached the
Chilterns in Buckinghamshire in the 1890s and soon after-
wards the railway company was promoting the idea of living
and walking in the countryside. This is real Metroland — a
name used on the railway's own publicity posters from 1915
and immortalised by Evelyn Waugh and John Betjeman. In
1919 Metropolitan Railway Country Estates Ltd was formed
to design, build and sell houses near the tracks to boost the
daily commuter traffic. There were Pullman cars running into
the City and even a Pullman car attached to the 11.35pm from
Baker Street to serve supper to those returning from the West
End theatres. Locomotives were named after such famous Chiltern figures as Oliver Cromwell, William Penn and John Milton.

This Walk is between stations at the end of London Transport's Metropolitan Line — British Rail trains from Marylebone use the same line and still run to Aylesbury as did the
Great Central Railway which called this 'the Line of Health'.
The Walk follows the tiny River Misbourne and the Buckinghamshire—Hertfordshire border through villages associated
with Cromwell, Milton and Penn.

Underground trains run, above ground, from Baker Street to
Amersham and Chorleywood. There is also an hourly British
Rail service from Marylebone Station (Monday to Saturday).

Amersham Station is at Amersham-on-the-Hill. Turn left
out of the station and at the bottom of the hill go left again
under the railway bridge. (Those leaving the station by the
'down' entrance should turn right on to a narrow footpath
which follows the line to the railway bridge.)

131

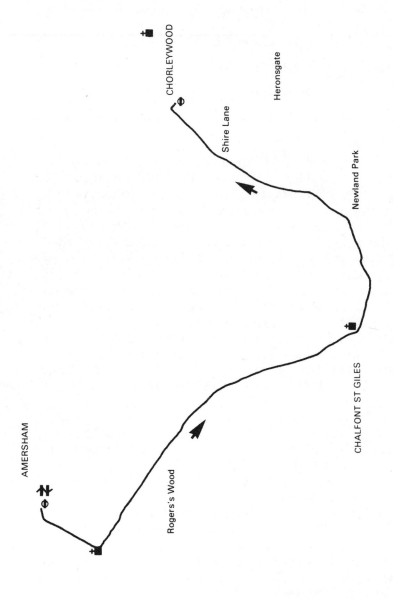

AMERSHAM

CHORLEYWOOD

Heronsgate

Shire Lane

Newland Park

CHALFONT ST GILES

Rogers's Wood

N

Walk 14 **THE CHILTERN HILLS**

Cross the road (under the bridge) and follow a metalled footpath along the bottom of the railway embankment (right). Before the end of the short path, bear left on to a woodland path which curves to follow a road (right). The road disappears as the path runs deeper into Parsonage Wood and begins to run downhill. The way becomes metalled just before emerging from the wood at the top of the hill. Below there is a panoramic view of Amersham. Continue down the path which curves round the wall of St Mary's Cemetery. Before reaching the cemetery's entrance turn right to cross the tiny River Misbourne and enter the churchyard. Go left to reach The Willow Tree tearooms (open daily except Mondays) in the Market Square.

At The Willow Tree turn left to follow the street south. Walk on the right-hand side of the road to pass The Griffin. (Look at the notice issued by magistrates in 1811 warning against 'Common Beggars, Ballad Singers and other Vagrants' on the front of number 60 London Road, once the first house in the town.) Cross the bottom of Gore Hill to pass Bury Farm (right)

AMERSHAM. The church is partly twelfth-century and has a fifteenth-century tower. The Victorian font was recently changed for a medieval one resembling the original which was removed in the nineteenth century. The impressive Drake Chapel belonged to the Drakes of Shardeloes — their mansion on a hill to the north-west is by Robert Adam. William Drake erected the Drake Almshouses (for six poor women) in the High Street in 1657 and his nephew gave the Market Hall in 1682. The much restored King's Arms Hotel is the ideal Elizabethan coaching inn. Cromwell's troops were billeted at The Griffin. William Penn, the founder of Pennsylvania, regularly visited his future wife at Bury Farm (below Gore Hill) just before their wedding (*see above*). The Willow Tree tearooms (*see above*) are part of the old Amersham Grammar School. Since the early thirteenth century an annual fair has been held along the High Street on 19 and 20 September during the parish patronal festival.

Amersham Market House

and turn right at the side of Bury Cottage. Bear left behind the cottage and head for the iron farm gate.

Cross a wooden stile at the side of the iron gate and walk ahead up the long field. A thin strip of Rogers's Wood comes down almost to the field boundary (right). Still keep ahead as the field opens out and at the far end (but not in the field corner) cross a stile. Continue ahead by the hedge (right). Soon after crossing a farm track, the hedge falls away and the path continues in the open. After passing farm buildings over on the far side of the field (left) the way becomes fenced on the left and then crosses a stile. Continue with the wire fence and, after a further stile, the fence ends to reveal a view of the (unreachable from here) Ivy House pub. Where the Misbourne (left) flows near to the way bear a quarter right to follow the foot of a rising bank in the field. Ahead (and not in the field corner) there is a wooden stile. Climb over the stile and walk ahead towards a solitary telegraph pole to find a wooden stile leading on to a metalled lane.

To the right there is a view of Lower Bottom House Farm. Cross the lane and go over the stile almost opposite. Follow the hedge (left) to cross another stile and walk ahead across a very wide field to find a stile in the trees to the right of the pylon. Cross the wooden stile and follow a path through the trees on the edge of a wood for just over ¼ mile. On emerging into the open the path widens to meet a road at a double bend. To the left there is The Old Mill.

Go ahead on to the road and keep forward on to a gravel path while the road bears left to ford the Misbourne. Beyond an isolated bungalow (right) the path becomes enclosed and enters a wood. Soon this path joins an exceptionally wide woodland way which runs past a few houses to the centre of Chalfont St Giles.

Cross the road to go under an arch next to the newsagent. Keep past the church gate (left) on an enclosed path which follows the churchyard round a double bend. Do not go over the stile (right) but keep ahead through the kissing gate and over the Misbourne footbridge.

Walk ahead on the worn path across the meadow to another

Chalfont St Giles

kissing gate which leads to a narrow path enclosed by tall wooden fences. Go up the path to a main road. Cross the road to find the start of another narrow footpath between The Edge (left) and the drive to Outlook (right). The narrow hedged way runs gently uphill. As the path flattens out there are some recently completed houses seen through the trees and bushes (left).

Where the path divides do not take the long straight path but go over the stile to follow the left fork. Bear left with the

---

CHALFONT ST GILES, in the Burnham Hundred, is part of the famous Chiltern Hundreds. Sir Robert Peel and Roy Jenkins are among the many Members of Parliament who have sought the now traditional appointment of 'Steward or Bailiff of Her Majesty's three Chiltern Hundreds of Stoke, Desborough and Burnham' so as to be able to relinquish membership of the House of Commons. The church, which is approached through an unusual lychgate, is usually open from 11.30am to 12.30pm and from 2.00 to 4.00pm. Inside there are monuments to the Fleetwood family who lived at The Vache (to the north of the main road). This was the home of Colonel Fleetwood who attended the Putney Debates (*see page 92*) and signed Charles I's death warrant. The house, which was named after the de Vache family from Normandy, later gave its name to Vache Island in the Indian Ocean when Sir Hugh Palliser, Captain Cook's friend, succeeded the Fleetwoods. John Milton came here in 1665 to escape the Great Plague of London and complete *Paradise Lost*. His cottage and garden (to the south in the main street) are open daily except Mondays, from 10.00am to 1.00pm and from 2.00 to 6.00pm between February and October; admission 60p, children 20p. Merlin's Cave, on the green, welcomes ramblers in the back bar which is reached by the side door. The Stratton Tea Rooms, opposite the village toilets, are open on weekdays. The street outside became the high street of Warmington-on-Sea for the making of the *Dad's Army* film, with The Crown as Captain Mainwaring's bank.

Misbourne ford

Milton's cottage

fences (left) to go through a gap and where the new low garden fence (left) ends keep forward across the field in a straight line to find a narrow gap in a hedge. Keep forward, with a glimpse of Ashwell's Farm (right), to cross a wooden stile in a second hedge. Turn right to follow the high hedge (right) and, after passing the end of a wire fence, go over a stile by an iron gate. On the right there is the entrance to Ashwell's Farm.

Cross the lane to go round an iron gateway (marked Rowan Farm) and follow the long straight woodland path for just over ¼ mile to meet another road opposite the entrance to Newland Park. Go through the gateway to pass the lodge (left).

Just past the lodge bear half left to cross a wooden stile at the side of the driveway. Bear half right over the field. The path, which tends to be well defined, passes near a field corner (right) and farther on stiles take the route across another corner (although walkers are tending to avoid the stiles). There is a view (right) of the old mansion before the path reaches an iron kissing gate.

Beyond the gate the fenced way passes between some of the open air museum exhibits before the path runs downhill to a stile on the corner of Shire Lane.

Turn left to follow the lane gently uphill. The left side, which was wooded until recently, is in Buckinghamshire whilst the right is part of Hertfordshire. The path rises in a cutting and at the top there are the remains of Philipshill Wood (left) where

---

NEWLAND PARK. The eighteenth-century house is now a college and part of the grounds have recently been given over to the Chiltern Open Air Museum. This is a collection of buildings, reflecting 500 years of local history, which have been saved from destruction and brought here. A baker's flour granary which once stood in Wing and the toll-gate and a chair-making factory from High Wycombe are among the structures which can be viewed closely or at a distance from the footpath. The museum, which welcomes visits from ramblers, is open Sundays and Bank Holidays between May and September from 2.00 to 5.30pm; admission 50p, children and pensioners 20p.

---

the trees grow in straight lines. Here the lane widens and there is a view of Bullsland Farm across the fields (right). On passing Piggy Lane (right) the way becomes metalled before meeting Heronsgate Road where there is through traffic.

Keep ahead down Shire Lane. Just beyond Chalfont Lane (left) there is Sunnybank (right) and a little farther on, The Orchard, which were both designed by Voysey (*see below*).

CHORLEYWOOD. The railway reached here in 1889 — three years before Amersham Station opened. The area was known as Chorley Wood from about 1730 and this original spelling is still occasionally used. The population was so small that the parish church was not built until the nineteenth century. The present building, on the north side of the Common, was designed by George Street but the tower is from the slightly earlier building by Benjamin Ferrey — the spire was added in 1881. W. H. Smith, the bookseller, subscribed to the rebuilding fund. Sir Henry Wood's wife and daughters used to worship here when he lived at Old Appletree Farm nearby. The main road by the church, surfaced only in 1914, was a turnpike road (as indicated by The Gate) which was once known as Gout Road since it had been built to enable Lord Salisbury to travel more easily from Hatfield to the Spa at Bath. In 1672 William Penn married his first wife at King John's Farm (on the corner of Shepherd's Lane) and later built a house in Pennsylvania to resemble the farmhouse. In 1846 Fergus O'Connor, the Chartist, laid out Heronsgate (to the south) as a co-operative village called O'Connorville. The scheme failed because the families resettled here were from the industrial north and lacked agricultural training. However, The Land of Liberty still stands just outside the model village — O'Connor disapproved of drink. Charles Voysey, the architect who was strongly influenced by art nouveau, lived at The Orchard in Shire Lane (*see above*) and also designed Sunnybank and Hill Cottage (now St John Fisher Church) in the same road.

Edward VIII post box

A rare Edward VIII post box stands near the corner of Haddon Road (right). Shire Lane runs gently downhill and, where the way becomes steep, passes the (easily missed) Church of St John Fisher on the right (*see page 139*). Go under the railway bridge and turn right for Chorleywood Station.

INDEX

141